Cracklin Bread
and
Asfidity

Cracklin Bread *and* Asfidity

FOLK RECIPES
AND REMEDIES
COMPILED BY

JACK SOLOMON
AND
OLIVIA PIENEZZA
SOLOMON

Illustrations by Mark Brewton

Introductions, Notes, and
Bibliographic Excursus
by the Compilers

THE UNIVERSITY OF ALABAMA PRESS
Tuscaloosa and London

Library of Congress Cataloging in Publication Data

Main entry under title:

Cracklin bread and asfidity.

1. Folk medicine—Alabama—Formulae, receipts,
prescriptions.   2.   Cookery, American—Alabama.
I.   Solomon, Jack, 1927–   II.   Solomon, Olivia,
1937–
GR110.A2C73   615'.882   77-13065
ISBN 0-8173-0724-9

First Paperback Edition 1993

Contents

Foreword

The Solomons, with obvious love and equally obvious diligence, have assembled a collection of folklore that is massive, eclectic, and joyful. In their own words, they did it because they wanted to recapture "a feeling of home." They reached out for all that made their place special, interesting, and dear.

They have preserved as much of it as they could in these volumes.

What the people of southeast Alabama clothed themselves in—in words and songs, in admonitions and jokes, in superstitions and recipes—was in no sense grand. It was not even original, but rather a medley from time immemorial. Yet it tied them to all that had gone on before them—and to each other. It soothed, humored, diverted, reminded, and ultimately saved them when "progress" passed them by.

And now when progress visits their children with new industries and the latest fashions from New York, perhaps it will save us again. It is no accident that this turn home comes at a time when our culture is being tested by an economic transformation unprecedented in the twentieth-century South. And even as we are drawn along, we are right to sense that such growth has its price in our resources, natural and human. More the reason to remember the communities and their ancient bonds that sustained us and made us more thoughtful, more sensitive, more compassionate—richer in every sense—than we would have been without these recipes and remedies, rhymes and riddles, songs and recollections.

University, Alabama   DAVID MATHEWS

Preface

Cracklin Bread and Asfidity, a collection of Alabama folk recipes and remedies, is the first of a number of volumes in which the full range of Alabama folklore will be surveyed. The scope, diversity, and strength of our folk traditions—legends, tales, narratives, songs, superstitions, games, rhymes, proverbs, riddles, and songs—will, we think, come as a pleasant surprise to our readers. This heritage cannot be other than a source of pride and joy for all Alabama folk. The materials of this and forthcoming volumes draw upon field studies made by Troy State University students, 1958–1962; field reportings from students at Alexander City State College, and neighbors, friends and family, 1970–1977; and upon the hitherto largely neglected collections made by workers in the Alabama National Writer's Project, Folklore Division, of the Works Progress Administration, 1936–1939.

Originally, we intended to publish these gatherings in archival volumes, but increasingly it became evident that here was treasure, a folk tradition so various, so vital, and so important that it deserved interpretation, explanation, and comment, particularly for young people, who, though daily forging a new folklore from the old, had never seen a battling stick or a smoothing iron except as a decorative device. The introductions, bibliographical aids, and notes are all designed to help readers recognize and understand the patterns that underlie a folk experience and to quicken their awareness of folklore as an expression of our history, our culture, and our character. This intent will be further augmented, throughout the volumes, by the musical notations of Miss Sarah Scott, and by the fine illustrations from Mark Brewton, whose eye and hand stir the folk memory and kindle the folk spirit.

The list of contributors appended to *Cracklin Bread and Asfidity* includes all known informants and collectors whose gatherings and reports have assisted the editors. Regrettably, over the past two decades, some names have been lost, and we offer our heartfelt apologies to any of those whose names do not appear.

Our folk heritage has shaped us, in large measure determined our response to our fellowmen and to our world. All of us participate in folk life, experience it from the moment of birth until our deaths. We are at the point in our nation's history when we have begun, in many novel ways, to explore our past: arts and crafts festivals, bazaars, and do-it-yourself kits are everywhere in evidence, and we are collecting things that remind us of times gone by, from wash pots to mule harnesses. All this points to a profound need in modern man. The study of folklore helps us know ourselves.

Perhaps the sense of alienation that afflicts so many city dwellers has arisen, in part, from the loss of community, of a place on earth we can call home. It is this sense of place, of identity carved from a definite landscape, that we feel so strongly in our folk traditions. Closely allied with art, history, sociology, literature, philosophy, religion, even medicine, folklore is none of these; rather, a vast body of concepts, knowledge, skills, poetry, and wisdom, evolving from a collective folk mind, transmitted orally, bodily, from generation to generation in peculiar forms—riddles, rhymes, sayings, and proverbs; remedies, and superstitions; tales and songs; crafts, arts, and skills; and festivals, customs, rites, and celebrations. And in all these, there is the feeling of home.

The folk traditions preserved in these volumes and in the others to come were given to us and our student collectors in good faith, with simple courtesy, freely, generously. Over the eighteen years of our marriage, they have haunted us. In all the splendid business of going to school, teaching school, setting up housekeeping, and raising our children, the spectre returned. No matter how often or strongly we pushed it aside for some other imperative or favorite, it came back. For five years we have lived with it daily, and now we think the revenant has come home to stay. So we give back the gift to our readers, who will find here a way of life that still exists in our hearts—a fragment of an old song, a yellowed page from an album, a tale told at the hearthside, a rime chanted fifty years ago in a schoolyard, a game we played at dusk, charming, bittersweet reminders of the past of our day-after-day, season-after-season, year-after-year life on this earth.

Our efforts in these volumes
are dedicated to our families
and our children.

Cracklin Bread

ALABAMA FOLK RECIPES

vanilla wafers

14

$\frac{1}{4}$ lb of butter

1 cup of sugar

1 egg

$\frac{1}{2}$ cup flour

2 or 3 tablesp. cocoa

1 ts vanilla flavoring

$\frac{1}{2}$ or 1 cup of nut meats

((◐⟩◑◐◐◯◐◯◐◯◔◒◒⌢☺)⟩☾◑((◑((◐◑◯◐◐◯◐◯◔◒◒⌢☺)⟩☾◑(

The South is legend—legend begetting legend. Never doubt it. And
though our great writers—William Faulkner, Eudora Welty, Carson
McCullers, Katherine Anne Porter, Thomas Wolfe, Reynolds Price,
Truman Capote, Flannery O'Connor, James Dickey, Shelby Foote,
James Agee, Willie Morris—have illuminated the legend, the Southern
mythos is, perhaps, ultimately inexplicable. As in all myth, truth holds
fast at the center: We *are* hospitable, our women *are* beautiful, and our
men *are* gallant and brave. And a whole lot of other things, all wildly
improbable and richly contradictory. Whatever else the world has
thought of that fabulous land below the Mason-Dixon line, it has
granted us one supreme achievement—Southern cooking, which, like
the South herself, is not one but many. The number of cookbooks on the
market purporting to be Southern is astounding. In fact, cookbooks
outsell everything but the Holy Bible, and when the recipes that
appear in monthly periodicals are added, the printed matter on cooking becomes staggering. Milady reels with the burden—casseroles,
cakes, pies, salads, whole meals whirl with hurricane force through
her brain.

Once, however, it was not so. A girl learned to cook from her grandmother and her mother—mostly by the "pinch and bit" method. A
pinch of this, a bit of that—more explicit directions were often mea-
sured in terms of fistfuls, hen eggs, and teacups. Sometimes an especially treasured recipe was committed to writing as a keepsake or for
swapping out with a neighbor. There is nothing quite like happening
on an old recipe among letters and diaries: the signature of a whole
lifetime, the flavor of a century, the feeling of times and places and folk
long buried, all there in the very handwriting and the yellowed paper.

Our student collectors were extremely successful in gathering recipes. Everybody, it seemed, had one. It is a rare woman who is not
flattered when a happy guest asks for the "receipt" of her dish. And
that pleasant custom persists, though some ladies used to prize recipes
so much that they refused to divulge their secrets. Real secrets were
few, and most women cooked the same foods in the same basic manner
as their neighbors; yet every cook had her own personal stamp. She
might be famous for small, thin, rolled, cut, crusty biscuits, or for
large, high, fluffy ones. One fellow told us recently, "I generally like a
biscuit with a heap of crumb to it. Can't sop syrup and gravy with them
little old bitty ones." Because of these subtle personal differences,
there is really no way to present a cookbook of traditional folk
recipes—so much depends on the manner of cooking, even the gestures

of rolling dough in a cupped palm or on a tabletop. For a comparable reason, the recipes are given essentially in the form in which they were taken down from the folk, to stress their authenticity, even where this involves some peculiar spellings and expressions, and a number of other irregularities in the words and abbreviations for units of measure, utensils, etc. And so we regard our gathering of recipes as a collection of folk material rather than an all-purpose cookbook of the "store-bought" kind.

Ours is certainly not a definitive collection, but it does represent the folk cooking of southeast and central Alabama in actual foodstuffs commonly available and found most often on everybody's table and in the most widely used methods of preparation. The geographical boundaries of these recipes are indicated by, among other things, the relative dearth of seafood recipes—the famous chowders, gumbos, and ocean fish feasts of Mobile and the Gulf area. Certain social, historical, and economic factors may clearly be observed here:

1. These are the recipes of, for the most part, white, middle-class, rural and small-town Alabama folk. This is certainly not to suggest that Negroes have not helped to create our particular folk cookery. Indeed, they have. By sheer happenstance, however, few of our informants were Negroes. We have all partaken literally of the same bread, though we have not always sat together at the same table. Foodstuffs and their preparation in Alabama have, historically, known few racial barriers, though there are some well-known major exceptions.

2. Folk recipes in Alabama, transmitted both orally and in writing, have come down to us virtually unchanged over the past one hundred or more years, and they are still in actual use. Certain economic forces—mainly mass production, improved transportation, and the specialization of agriculture—have produced some, but surprisingly not overwhelming, modifications in traditional Alabama cooking; and mass media have brought in ethnic, regional, and international influences. The core of traditional folk cooking, however, still flourishes.

3. Alabama folk cooking is directly related to the land itself, its climate, its botanical and zoological varieties, both domestic and wild. In a very real sense, the history of our agriculture may be read in this collection.

4. Although few of the recipes were taken down in the language of the informant, much of our folklife is discernible in the bare bones of instructions and ingredients, in the kinds and varieties of dishes and foods.

5. A fairly distinct portrait of the nineteenth-century housewife may be drawn from these pages: resourceful, thrifty, industrious, physically strong and agile, imaginative, deeply concerned about the welfare of her family, often wise and humorous, accepting her bounden

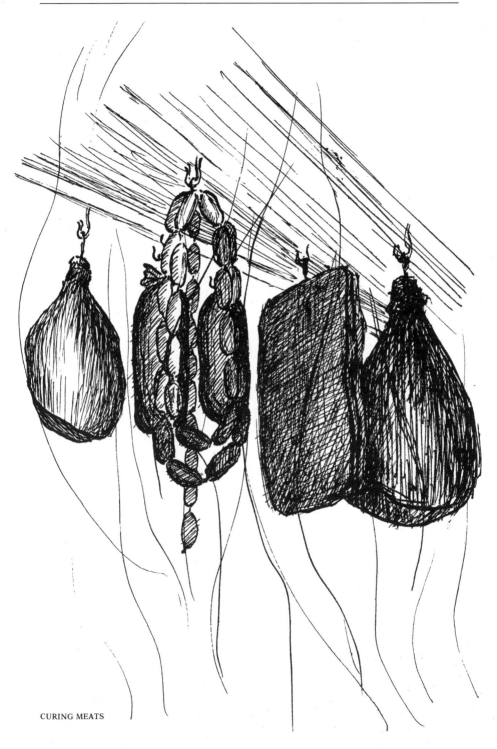

CURING MEATS

duties with cheer and wit, willing to rise early and go to bed late, creating much out of little, all in the good time of the season, and, in spite of countless obstacles, bringing to her table and home, loveliness, grace, and goodness. At the risk of offense in some quarters, we might say that it is unfortunate, somehow a bit saddening, that we do not now always prize the virtues of a good housekeeper. To some, her portrait may seem faded, ludicrous, even absurd; but we need to remember that she brought us through times as hard and dangerous as those we now face.

Traditional recipes are derivative; they derive from folk crafts and domestic arts—that is, they are the end result of all the year-long processes of planting, growing, and harvesting food. The contemporary supermarket gives us instant gratification; we choose whatever we please, go home, open the package or can, thaw and heat or, at the most, snap the beans, peel the potatoes, and cook the roast. For our grandparents, most foods were seasonal, and the methods of preserving, smoking, salting, drying, and canning were tedious and fraught with error, yet succeeding far more than they failed. Rural and even town households were self-sustaining. Town dwellers kept cows, hogs, and fowl, maintained fruit trees and small vegetable gardens, and had fairly easy access to food peddlers from the country. Their menfolk hunted and brought home squirrel, rabbit, possum, birds, and fish. The raising of food for his family was as important to the farmer as his cash crop. A recipe for chicken pie or pickled pig feet is inseparable from the processes that preceded it: catching the chicken, wringing its neck or chopping its head off, plucking, singeing, and dressing it. Hog-killing, lye-hominey making, preserving jams and jellies, distilling liquors and wines, are crafts in their own right, comparable to quilting, embroidery, weaving, and the domestic arts of the blacksmith and furniture maker.

In all these crafts, it is the feeling and proof of honest workmanship, of skill and inventiveness in the teeth of necessity and, often, sheer deprivation, of wit, courage, and determination, which impresses us so deeply today. These are the very qualities absent from so many articles manufactured in assembly-line production, particularly noticeable in commercially prepared foods. Of course, we do a good many things better than our grandparents did. Foods are safer and we know more about good nutrition, though our knowledge does not guarantee sensible diets. The folklorist who longs for the past, despises the present, and prophesies doom for the future is a bit of a fool, but every so-called improvement has an ancillary loss. With food, far too often, the loss has been taste.

Nearly every town has its own cookbook. Various organizations of Alabama's clubwomen often publish an inexpensive volume of recipes, and such publications sometimes contain a folk recipe. Katherine Tucker Windham's *Treasured Alabama Recipes* (Huntsville, Alabama: Strode Publishers, 1972) is a welcome addition to the cookbook library. The most useful and wide ranging of Alabama cookbooks is *Favorite Recipes of Alabama Vocational Home Economics Teachers*, sponsored by the Alabama Association of the Future Homemakers of America, first edition published in 1958. While it does not contain folk recipes per se, it presents a broad collection of foods we have enjoyed for over a century.

Old diaries, newspapers, and letters sometimes contain authentic folk recipes in their entirety and references to folk cooking. Mrs. Ruth Herren's recipe for pepper hash came from a letter written by her sister in the 1890s. Reprints of early American cookbooks are excellent guides to the tables of our ancestors. One, in particular, has given us great pleasure: *Housekeeping in Old Virginia*, an exact reprint of a volume edited by Marion Cabell Tyree and published in 1879 at Louisville, Kentucky, by John P. Morton, reissued by the Cookbook Collectors Library. Endorsements for the book were penned by the wives of illustrious men, governors and senators, and the wife of President Rutherford B. Hayes. As a cookbook, it is superb, covering every segment of this "domestic art" with specific, detailed instructions for bread- and cake-making, the cooking of vegetables, methods of preservation (including those for pickles, jams, jellies, and marmalades), and the slaughter, curing, and dressing of pork and fowl. There are, in addition, sections on dusting and cleaning, care of the sick, medicines and remedies, and directions for making items such as ink, lotion, and hair tonic. Here is an example of folklife set forth in articulate, lucid, published language, fit and proper for investigation by both the historian and the folk scholar. Lines of demarcation, once believed quite clear, blur, and interdisciplinary methods now emerge as imperatives for those who would chart the future of folk culture as a study worthy of our best minds and warmest hearts.

By and large, the best way to get hold of an authentic folk recipe nowadays is to talk with men and women over fifty. Fifty years may, at first glance, seem too young, but there is a remarkable continuity in traditional folk cooking, and though we are all happy, albeit sometimes decidedly unhappy, twentieth-century supermarket cooks, Alabama folk still bake biscuit and cornbread, boil turnips and collards, fry chicken (real and "Georgia" style), stir up pound cake and fruitcake, and now and then even make corn-meal gruel and 'tater' custard. And *one* of the legends about the South we swear is of absolute and enduring truth—the excellence of traditional Alabama folk cooking.

((()C()O⊙♉☺)()((

Beverages

The principal beverages of an Alabama household late in the nineteenth century were sweet milk, buttermilk, coffee, and tea.

Tea and coffee did not make their appearance in England and continental Europe until the latter half of the seventeenth century. The first printed reference to tea in English is found in an advertisement of 1658, and Samuel Pepys records his first taste of this pleasant drink in his famous diary (1660). The first license for coffee in the American colonies was issued in 1670, and a coffee house, that interesting social and literary phenomenon of seventeenth and eighteenth century England, was first founded in the new world in 1689. The importance of tea to the American colonists is well known: the Boston Tea Party helped rouse the spirits of the dissidents and the War for Independence was not long in coming.

In general, frontier Alabamians preferred coffee to tea as a table drink, though both were prized for their medicinal uses. With the advent of ice houses in Alabama towns during the early twentieth century and, later, of ice boxes and refrigerators, iced tea became, along with Coca-Cola, a Southern obsession. Country folk weren't so lucky—ice was available only on Saturday, the day for going to town; great twenty-five and fifty pound blocks hauled home in the wagon. Coffee, a necessary staple like flour and sugar, was purchased green, roasted, ground in a mill, and boiled, the residue sinking to the bottom—the end result being a drink so strong that it "could get up and walk," so pungent that one was lured from beneath a half ton of quilts down an icy hall or dogtrot to the only warm place in the house, so powerful that it waked the sleepiest of heads, and so good that it defies all telling.

Though we have no written recipes for coffee as a meal in itself, countless informants told us of dipping hunks of cheese in coffee, of dropping a raw egg into the boiling liquid, of crumbling up a biscuit in a cup of coffee, heavily creamed and sugared, a food often served to lap babies and children. Mrs. Drew Bailey's recipe for "Sure-Enough Biscuits" gives explicit directions for a "usual breakfast": eggs, ham, and sausage or side bacon, grits and gravy, butter, jelly and preserves, coffee, and sweet milk. And, she adds, put in "a baker of peanuts" or "maybe some sweet potatoes" after you take the biscuits out of the oven. A rural Alabama breakfast table often was laid with fried chicken, squirrel, rabbit, partridge, or even tenderloin and spare ribs during hog-killing time.

Every family had a milk cow—sometimes several—and woe-be-unto-us if the cow went dry. Some readers will remember the churn pushed up to the fireplace in winter, the wooden butter molds or presses, and gallon jugs of milk kept cool in the spring. Milk was served at every meal, there being some who swore by buttermilk, others who would have only sweet milk. We have heard it said that if you drink sweet milk with collards or turnip greens instead of buttermilk, you will assuredly die before sunup.

Festive occasions, weddings, and other celebrations required "punch"—usually alcoholic. "Ratifia" calls for brandy, wines, a pint of rose water, and a thousand peach kernels. Beers, wines, ciders, nectars, and whiskeys were common, and fabulous "possets" and "nogs" were a regular part of Christmas observances. The illicit distilling of wines and whiskeys is one of the enduring legends of Southern life and letters; every once in a while a sheriff still breaks up an illegal distillery, but the moonshiner and the bootlegger are a vanishing species. Whatever the scruples of conscience about whiskey as an intoxicant, most households kept a bit for medicinal uses. A Methodist minister visiting one of his ailing flock who was troubled by a wretched cough, confessed, shamefaced, that he lately had such an affliction and tried every cure, to no avail, until at last he lit on whiskey and rock candy and, thanks be, "That done it!"

Parched Coffee

Put whole grains of coffee in a long, shallow pan. Have the stove oven hot. Put coffee in the stove and stir ever so often. When coffee has browned and is parched, take the white of an egg and stir in the coffee.

The egg whites glazes the coffee. Then grind the coffee in a coffee mill (usually hanging on the wall in the kitchen) as needed. This makes good coffee and the grounds will stay in the bottom of the pot if the egg white has been used.

Mrs. C. T. Livingston

Coffee

Fill a wash pot full of water, set it over a long fire and let it simmer a while. Put coffee in cloth bags and throw into wash pot. Stir with a hickory stick. Boil and boil. (It is said that if you put your finger in the coffee you will make a hole in it, the coffee is so strong.)

Charlie Caddali

Editor's Note: Old timers report drinking "Acorn" coffee in lean times. Acorns were boiled in water until the liquor turned brown.

Sassafras Tea

1.
When you get the roots of the sassafras tree, scrub them carefully. The small roots are usually better than the large ones. Put water into a pan and let it boil. When the water boils put the roots in. Boil until the strength is like you want it.

2.
One half cup of roots
Two quarts of boiling water

Directions: Bring water to a boil and then drop in the roots.

Mrs. J. M. Moore

Note: Sassafras tea was generally used as a medicine, but was not unknown as a beverage.

Corn Whiskey

2 bushels corn
2 gallons syrup
10 gallons water

Let stand 5 to 8 days. Strain, remove corn then combine with 10 gallons of syrup and 50 gallons of water till it works off [ceases fermentation].

'Stilling

Cap the barrell with a wash pot airtite. Put a pipe into it. Turn it up side down, the pipe on top. Run the pipe through some water in a trough. Build a fire under the barrell and the steam that's running through the pipe is whiskey. This will make 4 gallons of whiskey.

Frankie McCarty

Corn Beer

One gallon corn. Boil and put in bag or 4 or 5 gallon jug. Add 1 gallon syrup to four gallons water. Let it set until it works off.

Clarence Kirkland

Fig Wine

Wash and mash 1 gallon of figs. Add 2 gallons of cold water. Put in crock jars and let stand and ferment 3 days. Then drip and strain. To every gallon of juice add 3 pounds of sugar. Let stand and work thoroughly for 10 days.

Blackberry Wine

Process: Mash 15 quarts of berries. Add 2 quarts cold water and let stand 3 days. Strain through a bag and to each 3 pints juice, allow 5 pints warm water and 3 pounds sugar. Dissolve sugar in warm water and when cold, add to juice. Fill jugs and as it works off, fill with water for a week and then cork lightly until it ceases to ferment, when it can be corked and sealed.

Mary Ann Wiley

Pokeberry Wine

Put alternate layers of berries and sugar in a loosely covered container. Strain and seal after the mixture has "worked off." (Pretty in a bottle but not recommended as safe.)

Reconstructed from a conversation
with Mr. Reuben Plant

Nectar

2 gallons berries (ripe)
50¢ worth tartaric acid

Wash berries and put in a stone crock. Dissolve tartaric acid in a quart of warm water and pour over berries. Let set 48 hours, strain and mix 2 cups of sugar to one cup of juice. Put in bottles and cork.

Note: Nectars were made from nearly any berry, even fruits such as plums, scuppernongs, and grapes.

Eggnog

1 egg   1 level teaspoon sugar
⅔ cup milk   1 tablespoon rum, whiskey, or brandy

Separate white from yolk—beat yolk and add sugar and milk. Stir in rum, whiskey or brandy and beat. Add stiffly beaten white at last moment before serving.

Mrs. A. L. Patterson

Custard Posset

One of the earliest Possets—a thick type of eggnog served hot.

14 eggs	½ lb. sugar
12 tablespoons sack (sherry wine)	Little nutmeg
9 tablespoons ale	1 qt. cream

Beat eggs well; add wine and ale; add sugar. Set mixture on coals (low heat) and stir until it begins to thicken. Add grated nutmeg to taste. Scald the cream and pour (slowly) into the egg mixture, cover and let stand for half an hour, then serve it up.

Mrs. T. D. Neely

Apple Juice

Beat up apples in a half flour barrel, with a maul. Have a hole (bung hole) near the bottom of the barrel with a peg stopper in it. The juice is drawn off and used as a drink. Use before apples have time to sour.

California Beer

Put California beer seeds into a jar of sweetened water-use syrup—let stand a few days to ferment. Pour off drink but leave seeds in the same jar. Pour sweetened water over the same seed to make another jar of beer. The seeds keep multiplying. They were usually shared with neighbors.

Mrs. J. J. Beard

Milk Punch

Peel rind from four large lemons and steep for twenty-four hours in a quart of brandy or rum. Then mix with it a pound and a half of sugar, the juice of the lemons, two grated nutmegs, and a quart of water. Add a quart of rich whole milk, boiling hot, and strain the whole mixture through a cloth or jelly bag. May be used as soon as it is cold, or it may be bottled and kept for several months.

Hattie Mae Mills

Rum Punch

One lemon, one glass of rum, thirteen glasses of water, either hot or cold, and sugar to taste; squeeze the lemon and pare it thin, mix well with the sugar and water, and then add the rum.

"Ratifia"

Take 1 gallon best brandy
1 quart madeira wine
1 quart muscat wine
1 pint orange-flavor water

3 pounds loaf sugar
1 pint rose water
1,000 peach kernels

Put in a crock and keep in sun for 4 or 5 days.

Mrs. Ernst

Muscadine Wine

5 lbs. of muscadines
5 lbs. of water
5 lbs. of sugar

Take 5 lbs. of muscadines and bust them up—put in churn—add the water; put 1 or 2 lbs. of sugar in to begin with. Let it work off until it quits working. Strain, then add remainder of sugar. Let stand for 14 days, or when it quits working. Put in bottles, leaving cap loose. After it has completely quit working, seal. Will have little bubbles around top.

Mr. Tommy Anderson

Scuppenong Wine

Now don't look to this not to fail you if you don't do like I tell you. An when I've done told you all I know, then, you still gotta have a sort o' feelin' about it, and if you ain't got that feelin', you just as good go buy your wine some 'eres, for you cain't make it.

Now you wash your scuppernongs the very same day you pick 'em. Don't you go pickin' 'em of an evenin' when the sun's low and the day's coolin', and then you go traipsin' off some 'eres, sayin', I'll start my wine come mornin'. You pick 'em fust off in the mornin', usin' a deep crock.

You can use a keg but a crock's better. Now you sprinkle sugar or honey over 'em. I cain't tell you now much, you jest sort of kiver 'em light like. Actually the honey's the best and I'd suggest flat-woods honey. Now you let 'em stand three to seven days, until they get a certain look. Now some folks say that when the time comes skim off the pummies. But that ain't my way. When it comes time, I put 'em in a flour sack and squeeze 'em. Then I put the juice back in the crock and add sugar real slow, and stir them gently. Put just enough sugar in it to make a egg float. Take it out right then and bottle it with the tops off and cover the tops with a cloth. Each day add a little more to the bottle for that which has shrunk. When it quits working, cork it and place it on its side in a dark place. Then you got some fine wine.

Rose Reynolds

Scuppernong Wine

Gather the fruit ripe. Bruise them without breaking the seed. Put them into an open vessel and cover with a cloth. This three times in the first 24 hours. Let it stand three days.

Press out the juice, strain through a flannel cloth or bag. Add sugar until it will float an egg to the surface.

Put into jugs, filling them and leaving the mouths unstopped—reserving a bottle of the juice to replace that which escapes from the jugs by fermentation.

When fermentation ceases, strain, and put into clean jugs, cork the jugs tightly and set in a cool place where they will not be disturbed until 1st of November.

(Be sure fermentation has ceased before you cork tightly, or your jug will burst.)

Mrs. J. R. Burnett, Jr.
through a letter to
Mrs. Mary Americus Williamson
(Muddie Wishy)

Regent's Punch

¼ pound of rock candy
High grade green tea
1 bottle of champagne

½ bottle of sherry
1 lemon sliced
1 tumbler of brandy

Dissolve rock candy in approximately 1 pint of hot tea. When cold, add other ingredients—20 to 25 servings.

Mrs. Ernst

Breads, Doughs, Dressings, and Stuffings

We once knew a gentleman who ate cornbread with his pies, puddings, custards, and ice cream—said he couldn't abide sweets but couldn't stand to see anything go to waste, so he made them tolerable with cornbread. And a lady of our acquaintance says she can't ever make her meal come out even; she'll take a biscuit to finish off a piece of chicken and then she's got biscuit left, so she takes another piece of chicken—and so on. Another fellow eats biscuit or cornbread after dessert "to get the sweet out." But nobody needs a reason to eat Alabama biscuits and cornbread—they *are* a reason. There are as many ways to prepare them as there are cooks; but, in general, the breads of Alabama folk fall into two categories, based on the fundamental ingredients of corn meal or flour. These include:

Corn—Pone or skillet or fingerprint bread, made with water, salt, soda, and bacon drippings and baked in the oven; fritters fried in grease on top of the stove; egg bread, which features eggs and whole milk; cracklin bread, corn dodgers, hush puppies, and dressing for poultry.

Flour—Yeast breads, in loaf form or rolls, made with either yeast cakes or white potato "starter"; rolled or cut biscuits; dumplings for pies, both meat and dessert pies; and as dressing or stuffing.

Hoecakes, cooked either on top of the stove or in ashes (hence the name ashcake) may be either of corn or flour—useful when the cook is in a hurry. Sweet-potato biscuits are among the delicacies of Alabama cooking. They were often served on Sunday with sausage, ham, and tenderloin. Our informants yielded some lovely names for breads: Everlasting Bread, a reference to the "starter" with religious overtones; Chink-and-Dob, a term derived from chimney construction; and Pleasant Bread. Readers over forty will be familiar with a certain between-meal snack from a day when there were no candy bars or soft drinks—a syrupy hole biscuit from the warming oven of a wood stove.

"Sure-Enough Biscuits" (Grannie's Recipe)

Sift four handsfull of flour into the breadpan. Make a little hole in the middle of it, put you about 2 spoons of baking powder in it with about that much salt (indicating 1 spoon). Scoop up about a half handful of lard and put that in too.

Now mix about a cup of buttermilk (oversized cups) with some soda and pour into mixture. Mix it with hands and roll out biscuits. Put them into a hot wood stove oven for a few minutes and have everything else ready to eat.

Serve with usual breakfast: Eggs (fried and scrambled), ham and sausage or side bacon (hand sliced), grits and gravy, butter (real yellow) and jelly and preserves, coffee (black and strong with chicory) and sweet milk.

Put a baker of peanuts in the oven when you take out the biscuits. The children always like some to eat while they play. Or maybe some sweet potatoes.

Mrs. Drew Bailey

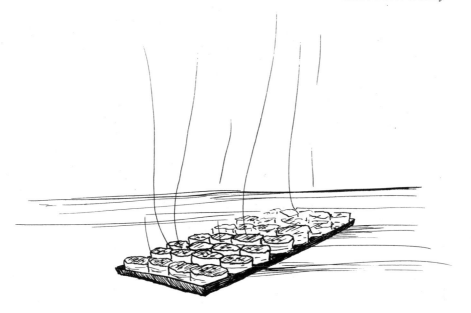

Beaten Biscuits

2 quarts of flour	1 pinch of baking powder
1 tablespoon of sugar	1 small cup of lard
1 teaspoon of salt	1 cup of cold milk
1 pinch of soda	

Sift soda, salt, and baking powder into flour, then work the lard in well. Add milk. Make up into a stiff dough, and work by beating until the dough pops like a shot. Cut and bake in a very slow oven.

Louise Jolly

Monkey Biscuits

Into skillet put two tablespoons butter and ½ cup molasses. Heat slightly, drop in split, day-old biscuits. Fry both sides. Serve hot.

Mrs. Maynard Tindall

Sour-Milk Biscuits

It takes a pint of sour milk, a quart of sifted flour, and a chunk of butter twice the size of a walnut. Rub the flour and butter together and add about a teaspoonful of salt; then mix this into the sour milk. Be sure to dissolve a teaspoonful of baking soda and stir this into the milk while you add the flour. Then you must knead up the dough quickly. Don't handle it too much. Roll out and cut with a biscuit cutter. Bake in a quick oven.

Sweet-Potato Biscuits

2 cups sifted self-rising flour	¼ cup cooked mashed sweet
3 tablespoons shortening	potato sweetened to taste
⅓ to ½ cup buttermilk	

Cut shortening into flour. Add buttermilk and mix. Add sweet potato and work in with hands.

Roll out on floured cloth. Bake at 425° until done. (I use an old cast-iron "baker" so they won't brown on bottom too fast).

Louise Jolly

Sweet-Potato Biscuits

⅓ portion of baked sweet potato
⅔ portion of flour

Use seasoning to taste
Mix with buttermilk

Bake in hot oven.

Mrs. A. B. Gantt

Sweet-Potato Biscuits

½ teaspoon soda
1 teaspoon baking powder
2 tablespoons lard
1 cup buttermilk

1 pinch of salt
2 cups of cooked mashed
  sweet potatoes

Knead all ingredients together and roll into round biscuits. Place on biscuit baker and bake until brown.

Mrs. Otis Walker

Brown Bread

Use meal—cook it in a boiler over another boiler of water to keep it from sticking.

Add 2 eggs
1 cup of syrup
nutmeg

After it begins to thicken up, put in oven and bake until golden brown.

Mrs. B. T. Tillman

Alabama Spoon Bread

4 eggs beaten separately
2 cups sweet milk
1 cup cooked grits
4 T. corn meal

1 t. sugar
1 t. salt or more
1 t. baking powder
1 T. butter

After mixing, bake in pan, inside of stove. Cover until set well, then remove cover and brown.

Mrs. Louise Jolly
and
Mrs. T. B. Nettles

Light Bread

Soak the dry rising (yeast) two hours, then mash the potatoes through a sieve, then add flour to the potatoes, and pour the water on, that the potatoes had been boiled in, and cool to lukewarm water to the consistency of yeast, and add yeast and let rise, then add flour and knead to dough and let it rise, then knead into pans and let it rise and put into the oven and bake one hour.

Light Bread

Fill half gallon bucket about ½ full of luke warm water, stir in single handful of meal, then stir in flour (if plain use a pinch of salt and a pinch of soda) 'til mixture is about like thick buttermilk, set this in a pan of lukewarm water and keep at same temperature. Drain off water that comes to top of mixture twice, but do not jar or stir the mixture. This should be put up at sunrise and should be made into dough at noon. Put mixture (yeast) into large tray of flour, knead and form into loaves, put in greased pan and let rise 'til double in bulk (keep same temperature as yeast was kept). When bread is double in size bake in hot oven for about 15 minutes then butter lavishly on top and bake at lower temperature 'til brown and seems done.

Mrs. C. F. Partridge

Old-Fashioned Light Bread

In the evening, break and dissolve 1 cake yeast in a pint of lukewarm water. Mix with 1 qt. flour to thick batter. Cover and let rise in warm place 7 or 8 hours, or overnight.

Early in the morning mix sponge with 1 pint lukewarm water, 4 teaspoons salt 4 tablespoons each, sugar and lard. Add about 2 qts.

flour. Mix to medium dough. Knead about 10 minutes and let rise until double again. Mold into loaves; Let rise to double size. Bake 45 to 60 minutes in moderate oven. Avoid becoming chilled.

Mrs. Willie Dismukes

Potato-Yeast Bread Or Everlasting Bread

1 pt. flour
½ pt. sugar
1 cake yeast

Sufficient lukewarm potato water to make a sponge. Keep in a warm place for two or four days or until it rises and fulls and is ready for use—this is the starter.

How to make the bread—take the starter and use one quart cold water and enough water and enough flour to make a rather stiff batter, and beat like you would a cake. (Let rise and take out one pint of sponge for next starter and put one cup of sugar over it and set in cool place). Add salt to rest of the sponge and mix as you would any yeast, work throughly, let rise, mold in loaves, let rise, and bake, the oftener this yeast is used, the better will be the bread. Bake in moderate oven about one hour.

Pauline Johnson

White-Potato Bread

Boil the potatoes. Put sugar, butter, and eggs in it. Bake in the oven until brown.

Mrs. Ashley Culver

Pleasant Bread

Take 2 dry yeast cakes, dissolve in qt. lukewarm water. Add 4 tablespoons sugar, ⅓ cup cooking oil and 1 tablespoon salt. Add (plain) flour until soft dough. Grate in all the cheddar cheese you can afford, stir in, cover with damp cloth, leave in warm place to rise 'til double in bulk.

To knead, pour mixture into large tray of flour, take palms of hands and turn and push dough around (don't let it know you're afraid of it).

Shape into loaves, place into thick greased pan, cover damp cloth and let rise 'til double in size.

Bake in 375 degrees oven 15 minutes, then butter tops lavishly and bake 'til brown.

Lady who cooks for the
Rotary Club at Andalusia

Yeast Bread

Take potatoes, cook and mash up. Let them set up and let them sour. Use this for yeast biscuits. Use lard, pinch of salt and soda in them. Knead your flour well and set them in the sun to rise.

Mrs. J. M. Thompson

Corn Sweet Bread

1 cup butter   1 teaspoon soda
1 cup buttermilk   1 egg
2 cups corn meal   ½ cup shortening

Mix ingredients well, flavor with grated orange peel and bake until a golden brown.

Mrs. Carrie Windham

Corn Dodgers

1 cup of meal   ¼ cup of chopped onions
¾ cup of hot water   ½ tsp. salt

Stir well 'till moist. Dip by spoonfuls into small round cakes and drop into boiling turnip juice.

Mrs. Mable Patterson

Corn Dodgers

Four cups of yellow corn meal, a teaspoonful of salt, a tablespoonful of melted butter. Mix into a soft dough with cold water. Make into patty-cakes and put in greased pans. Bake in hot oven until crust is brown. Serve hot.

Allen Blackstock

Corn Pone

Use a coarse meal. Add a dash of cream of tartar, baking soda, and a pinch of salt. Mix with buttermilk. Shape by hand into pones. Place in a well-greased warm iron skillet. Cover tops and sides with grease. Bake until a golden brown. Can be baked in loaf or muffin cups.

Allen Blackstock

Pone Bread

In large bowl or pan, make three piles of meal, about 1 cup to each pile. Poke a hole in center, put in ½ tsp. baking powder and ¼ tsp. salt, mix up lightly with fingers. To each pone add enough cold water to make stiff dough. Work up with hands. Put in greased skillet, best to use bacon fat, then pour grease over each pone. Bake in hot oven for 35 to 45 minutes or till brown. Add grease if you have to, turn pones once to make sure crust gets good and brown. Serve hot. Break off pieces with hands. Do not cut with knife.

Mrs. M. H. Solomon

Corn Bread

Put some fat into an iron skillet and into hot oven. Mix 3 parts corn meal to 1 part flour—just however much bread you want. Mix salt, baking powder, and buttermilk along with a little sugar (I put a little sugar in almost all my vegetables too, it brings out the proper flavor). Pour in some bacon drippings if you like it and put into the hot skillet. Bake for about 30 minutes while you dish up the other food. Serve cold buttermilk (with little pieces of butter left in).

For cracklin bread, add some baking soda and cracklins and leave out the bacon drippings. The cracklins will be greasy enough.

Mrs. Drew Bailey

How Hush Puppies Got Their Name

Men in the community would go fishing, bring big messes home, clean them and the wives would cook them at one house. Everybody would gather around large tables to eat. The dogs would smell the fish and bread cooking and begin to howl for their share. To keep them quiet, they were given some of the bread. This was to hush the puppies (and children too, I'm sure).

Chip onions into cornmeal, salt, baking powder, and water, roll into small balls and drop into hot grease where fish are frying or have been fried. When they rise to the top and are light golden brown, remove, drain and serve very hot. These go well with fresh hot fish.

Mrs. Drew Bailey

Crackling Bread

Take about a qt. of cornmeal and sprinkle a little bit of salt in it. Then mix about 2 handfuls of cracklings in it and work it up good by adding a little water. Make it with your hands and make it in pones. Bake until brown and serve with buttermilk.

Mrs. Elise House

Crackling Bread

Sift double handful corn meal
Put in pinch salt, pinch soda,
Single handful hog cracklins.
Pour in buttermilk and scrabble
With hands. Put in pan and bake.

Crackling Bread

One double handful of cornmeal   Five pinches of soda
Five pinches of salt   One handful of cracklings

Directions: Take a double handful of cornmeal, five pinches of soda, five pinches of salt, and add a handful of cracklings. Stir in enough buttermilk so you can pat it out in pones. Throw it in the oven.

Crackling Bread

2 cups cornmeal   1 cup sour milk or buttermilk
¼ teaspoon salt   1 cup crackling, diced
½ teaspoon soda

Louise Weeks

Note: Cracklings are bits of crisp, brown skin or rind of pork, left after rendering the fat during hog killing. Student collectors reported numerous crackling-bread recipes, all of them derived from, or similar to, this one. The contemporary recipes are, of course, characterized by specific measurements and instructions. The bread, loved by most Alabamians, is served hot with vegetables, especially collards and turnips at the main meal, cold at supper with the leftovers, hot at breakfast with syrup, sidemeat, tenderloin, sausage, or other pork dishes, and milk. Crackling bread and buttermilk is a meal in itself. Other contributors whose recipes for crackling bread are similar to these are: Mrs. Mae Reeves, Mrs. Laura E. Turner, Mrs. J. T. Brown, Mrs. T. J. Nicholas, and Mrs. Ora Wikle.

Crackling Bread

1½ cups cornmeal
½ teaspoon salt
2 tablespoons flour
1 egg, beaten

3 teaspoons baking powder
1¼ cups milk
1½ cups cracklings

Combine cornmeal, flour, salt, baking powder, egg and milk. Add cracklings. Beat thoroughly. Drop by teaspoonful on a hot, well-oiled griddle and fry until golden brown.

Mrs. W. R. Lidale

Crackling Bread

3 cups white corn meal
1½ cups cracklings (cut fine)

1 teaspoon salt
2 cups water

Mix corn meal, cracklings, and salt together. Add water and stir. Form into oblong cakes and place in greased baking pan. Bake in hot oven (450 degrees) for about 25 minutes.

Lilla Mae Griswold

Corn Muffins

Use a half cup of corn meal, a cup of flour, a cup of milk, two eggs, a medium tablespoonful of butter, 3 level tablespoonfuls of sugar, 3 teaspoonfuls of baking powder. Beat eggs together until light; add milk and sugar; then add flour, corn meal and butter, melted. Bake in a hot oven until golden brown.

Jimmie's Corn Muffins

4 cups corn meal
½ cup flour
1½ cups buttermilk
1 cup sweet milk
¼ cup shortening

½ teaspoon sugar
½ teaspoon salt
5 teaspoons baking powder
2 eggs, well beaten

Mix the dry ingredients. Stir in beaten eggs. Fold in oil. Stir in milk. Put batter in heated and greased muffin tins. Bake.

Jimmie Flowers

Pone Bread

Take 2 cups of corn meal, salt according to taste. Work into a stiff dough with water. Make large pone with hands. Put in well greased baker. Put lots of grease on top and sides. Bake in oven on medium heat until done.

Mrs. Lucy Chapman

Corn Sticks

2 eggs
2½ cups sifted meal
2 cups buttermilk
3 tablespoons melted fat

2 teaspoons salt
1 teaspoon sugar
1 teaspoon soda
3 teaspoons baking poweder

Mix and bake in hot oven.

Mrs. A. L. Patterson

Hoecake Bread

You add a dash of salt and a little bit of baking powder to some flour. Mix this up with water, just like you do with corn bread and fry it in a skillet, by just greasing the skillet. Don't put it into the oven to bake.

Mrs. Marilyn Clemmons

Hoecake Bread

4 cups of white cornmeal
2 teaspoons salt
boiling water

Mix the salt and cornmeal—pour enough boiling water in it to make it barely stick together. Grease a skillet with some grease and spread the mix in the skillet. Cook slow and when brown you turn it over to brown on opposite side. Serves about 12 people. May also be fried in patties.

Maggie Hart

Editor's note: Hoecake Bread is named for the manner of its cooking—on a hoe above the coals of a dying fire.

Rolls Rolls Rolls

¼ cup sugar   1 tablespoon lard
1 teaspoon salt   1 cup boiling water

Mix this and let cook to luke warm, then add:

1 yeast cake which has been dissolved
⅛ cup luke warm water
½ teaspoon sugar

Then add one beaten egg, pour in 2 cups flour, beat well. Add 2 more cups flour beat extra good, put in large buttered bowl and let rise.

Bake the rolls in a quick oven, brushing over butter before baking to brown them.

Mrs. Guy Wilson

Butter Rolls

Make biscuit dough. Roll out as large as you want it. Spread butter all over it. Sprinkle sugar and any kind of spice you prefer. Roll up as you would a jelly roll and cut in pieces. Put in a deep pie pan and cover with sweetmilk and bake until done.

Mrs. Sallie Seay

Chink and Dob

Four handfuls of sifted flour in wooden bowl. Add about 2 big pinches of baking powder and 1 pinch of soda. Add 2 handfuls of hog lard and 2 pinches of salt. Sweeten to taste (about one cup of sugar).

Mix thoroughly with hands and add buttermilk to desired dough for rolling out. Add more flour if needed. Put spiced apple sauce between layers and bake in oven until done.

Ruth Neely Parks

Pop-Overs

Use 2 cups of milk, 2 cups of flour, 2 eggs, one teaspoonful of butter, one teaspoonful of salt; mix to a batter and drop in cup-cake tins. Bake in a hot oven 12 to 15 minutes. Cover with a sweet sauce or cream, while hot.

Old-Fashioned Dressing or Cush

1 pone of cornbread
½ onion
2 tbs. bacon grease

Mix with water and cook 'til done.

Mrs. Virginia Eiland

Cush

Corn Bread   Spring Onion
Cold Biscuit   Eggs

Bake in moderate oven.

Miss Callie Ward

Boiled Apple Dumplings

You must make a rich biscuit (like baking-powder biscuit). Roll out
very thin and cut into sizes large enough to cover a whole apple. Peel
and cut apples in half. Lay two halves of apple on dough squares and
sprinkle with spoonful of sugar, pinch of cinnamon, and stick in one
clove. Pull up corners square and pinch together. Then take squares of
cloth, big enough to wrap each dumpling. Dip these in hot water and
sprinkle with flour. Wrap each dumpling in a cloth and drop in boiling
water for 45 minutes. They taste splendid when served with a sauce.
Some prefer them served with sweetmilk or cream.

Chicken Dressing

Take 8 or 9 left over biscuits. Soak in chicken broth. Take a handful of
corn meal, add to biscuit and broth with a large onion. Make up with
12 eggs. Use lots of chicken grease off the chicken broth. Cook in oven
until done through.

Mrs. Maye Price

Cornmeal Dumplings and Turnips

Cook turnips which have been seasoned with pork and salt until tender. Leave a large amount of water in the greens.

Mix fine cornmeal with salt and water. Shape by hand into patties. Drop the patties into the boiling water and turnips. Cook until dumplings are done.

Allen Blackstock

Chicken and Dumplings

Take one young chicken and put in a good size stew pot. Cook for about 9 hours and thirty minutes. Put a good bit of salt in the water that you are cooking the chicken in.

The dumplings are made just like bread. Take the dough and drop it in the pot in pieces about as long as your finger. Put enough butter in the pot to get little round drops on the top of the water. It should cook until the chicken begins to fall from the bones.

Willie Tate

Jumblies

Cream together two cupfuls of sugar and one of butter, add three well-beaten eggs and 6 tablespoons of sweet milk, two tablespoons of baking powder. Flavor to taste, enough flour to make into a soft dough; do not roll it out, but break off pieces about the size of a walnut and make into a ring by rolling them in rolls about the size of your finger and pinching the ends together. Put them in pans to bake—about an inch apart, they will rise and spread. Bake in a moderate oven until brown. These will keep a long time.

Elizabeth Berry

Turkey Stuffing

Take stale or very dry bread and cut off brown crusts (to make about a pound). Place in pan and pour lukewarm water over crusts. Allow to soak for a few minutes; then with hands squeeze out water and place moist crumbs in a large bowl. Add a teaspoon of salt, and pepper to taste, and about a teaspoonful each of savory, ground sage and minced herbs; then add a half cup of melted butter and a beaten egg. Stir thoroughly and stuff turkey. (For an 8 to 10 lb. bird)

((((🌑🌒◐○◑◐☉☽⌒☺)(🌓)((((🌑

Cakes, Cookies, and Candy

Every now and then a cake falls at our house. The cook is frustrate and irritable, but her husband and children are delighted with "the sad streak." Sad streaks are, lamentably, rare in these days of accurate ovens and electric mixers. The housewife of nineteenth-century America had few weapons against cake failure—a strong beating arm, a wooden spoon, an eccentric stove, and her own grit—yet she nearly always succeeded. A ninety-year-old neighbor told us her cakes always took a notion to fall when the preacher took dinner at her house. Another neighbor commented that she didn't care for cake much any more, "I reckon because I have it any time I want to." Like bread-making and washday, baking cakes was arduous, and though one might have cobbler pies and custards once a week or Sunday, the cake was reserved for special times: funerals, weddings, Christmas, and all-day-singing-and-dinner-on-the-ground.

The pound cake and teacakes dominate the recipes of this collection. Their supremacy may be attributed, in part, to the fact that the ingredients were usually on hand—flour, sugar, butter, and eggs. Spices and dried fruits for fruit cakes, wedding cakes, and Lane cakes were relatively hard to come by. A press for making powdered cocoa was not available in America until 1823, and thereafter commercial manufacture and distribution of milk chocolate and cocoa moved slowly. What we hold cheap today was dear enough a century ago. There are, however, everyday cakes—Sally Lunn, which calls for one or two eggs and little sugar, and which was baked as a tea muffin; and Sweet Bread or Cake, which was made with syrup and corn meal. Syrup and molasses were often used as substitutes for ground sugar. In sharp contrast is the wedding cake that requires 200 eggs, 20 pounds of butter, sugar, and flour, 40 pounds of currants, and 20 glasses of brandy! The two Alabama recipes for wedding cake that we collected are among the oldest in America.

Lane cakes and fruit cakes were an important part of the celebration of an Alabama Christmas. The basis of fruit cake is pound cake, which takes its name from the weight of its ingredients: a pound of sugar, butter, flour, and eggs, though, as these recipes indicate, a pound of something was not always available, or the cook might choose to vary the recipe. Beating up a pound cake by hand is hard work—there is a special technique for holding the bowl between the crook of the arm and the body and beating with the other hand. Truman Capote has written a beautiful account of Alabama fruitcake-baking in his story, "A Christmas Memory." The old lady in the story begins her preparations in November, before Thanksgiving, as did most housewives of that era. When the cakes are cool, they are wrapped in a clean flour sack, usually homemade, which is saturated in wine or whiskey and set in a cool, dark place. In the weeks before Christmas the flour sack is moistened with spirits several more times, and by Christmas the flavors are blended. The cakes can be kept this way for a year. The brilliantly colored candied fruits, the nuts, raisins, and spices are apt symbols of the season—treasures not unlike those of the Magi. A week before the holiday the housewife made more cakes—Lane, coconut, spice, nut, and pound cakes and set them in a cool place, the backporch or an unused, unheated guest bedroom or dining room, to keep against Christmas. Such extensive preparations appear right foolish today when the family has shriveled to one puny unit, but a century ago the family was not "immediate"; it included cousins to the fifth degree, and they all gathered at the home place to visit with each other and with friends and neighbors. On Christmas morning children and grown-ups in small towns and rural communities trooped from house to house, drinking eggnog and coffee, eating cake at every house. After the feast itself, there was the long afternoon, the women cleaning up and chattering in the kitchen, the men walking about the farm, the children at their everlasting play, the return to the table for supper, and, at last, eating nuts, apples, and oranges before the fire. There has never been anything like it since—those Christmases of our childhood.

In the days of the rolling store and the general store, a few candies were sold—peppermint, gum drops, vanilla cremes, licorice, and horehound. They were luxuries, usually eaten around Christmas time. Most candies were made at home—pecan and peanut brittle, divinity, taffy, all from syrup. Later, chocolate fudge joined the ranks of homemade candies, and it is still a favorite, even though it is apt to be concocted of confectioner's sugar, marshmallows, and ready-mixed cake frostings.

The variety of cookies available in a modern supermarket is almost unbelievable. In our grandparents' time there was one supremely delicious cookie—a short-bread teacake of English and European descent. They are difficult to make, requiring much time and patience, but they are worth all the effort. Every cook seems to have had her own recipe, and for that reason we have included several. Like gingerbread and plain muffins, the teacake is an everyday, any-day dessert. Their very commonness makes them special to the folklorist and to Alabamians who reached into the flour sack (in which they were stored) for a handful. Most cooks rolled them out small to medium-sized, but in some locales a saucer-sized teacake was popular. The editors have tested nearly all these teacake recipes; we are happy to say that our work was not wasted.

Apple-Sauce Cake

You need 1 cup of sugar; 1 cup of lard or butter, 2 cups of sweet apple sauce, 1 teaspoonful of soda (to be stirred into sauce). One teaspoonful of cinnamon, clove and nutmeg; 3½ cups of flour, one cup of raisins and 2 cups of nut meats.

Cream the butter and sugar; add the sauce and stir into the flour. Add the spices and nuts. Bake in good oven as a loaf cake.

Mrs. Rachel Peacock

Brown Betty

Grease a pudding dish and spread over the bottom a layer of fine bread crumbs and chopped apples. Sprinkle brown sugar, cinnamon and a bit of butter on each layer. Top off with crumbs. Pour half a cup of water over it and place in oven. Bake for an hour. Keep covered closely for the first half hour.

Brown Betty is best when served with hard sauce or cream. Tasty and very economical dessert.

Mrs. Rachel Peacock

Bible Cake

2 cups Jeremiah, chapter 6, verse 20,
1 cup Genesis, chapter 4, verse 4,
1 cup Judges, chapter 5, verse 25
4 of Isaiah, chapter 10, verse 14
4 cups of fruit of 1 Kings, chapter 4, verse 22
2 cups of fine 1 Samuel, chapter 30, verse 12

2 cups Nahum, chapter 3, verse 12
2 cups Numbers, chapter 17, verse 8
2 tsp. of 1 Samuel, chapter 14, verse 25
1 pinch Leviticus, chapter 2, verse 13
Add 2 tsp. of baking powder.

Mix as any other cake.

Mrs. O. S. Kilpatrick

Scripture Cake

1 cup Judges 5:25
2 cups Jeremiah 6:20
3 cups I Kings 4:22
3 tsp. Amos 4:5
A little Leviticus 2:13
Season with I Kings 10:2 to taste

1 cup boiling Genesis 24:11
1 cup Numbers 17:8
1 large spoonful Proverbs 24:13
6—Jobs 39:14
2 cups chopped I Samuel 30:12
2 cups chopped Rev. 6:13

Take Solomon's advice for making a good boy—mix and beat well. You will have a good cake. Proverbs 23:14

Tea Cakes

1 cup butter or shortening
1¼ cup sugar (1½ cup syrup)
3 cups flour
3 whole eggs

3 drops of vanilla or lemon
dash of salt
2 tbs. buttermilk

Louzina Rhodes

Tea Cakes

1½ teacup sugar
3 pieces of butter (size of an egg)
2 whole eggs
½ teacup sweet milk
1 dessert spoon baking powder

1 lb. sifted flour
60 drops vanilla
60 drops orange (extract—can substitute, peel lemon or orange)
60 drops lemon

Beat sugar, butter, eggs, milk and flavoring—add flour until dough looks like biscuit dough. Cut in shapes—cook until brown.

Mrs. Carrie Dendy

Tea Cakes

Take a lump of lard. Put in enough sugar according to how much you want to make. Add an egg. Mix a little flour. Keep adding until you can roll it out.

Mrs. A. D. Watkins

Tea Cakes

⅔ cups butter
1¼ cups sugar
2 eggs
1 teaspoon vanilla

1 tablespoon milk
3 cups flour
1 teaspoon salt
2 teaspoon baking powder

Roll out in desired shapes. Bake in a 375-degree oven.

Mrs. Rozelle Coxwell

Old-Fashioned Teacakes

⅔ cups syrup
¼ cup shortening
¼ teaspoon salt
1 teaspoon vanilla

1 egg
1½ cups flour
½ cup milk
2 teaspoons baking powder

Louise Weeks

Old-Fashioned Tea Cakes

¾ cup butter
¼ cup lard

Cream with two cups of sugar, 1 tsp. of lemon flavoring. Beat in 3 eggs—1 at a time. One tablespoon of milk, 2 tsp. of baking powder to enough flour to roll out thin. Cut out and roll out thin, or pinch off and pat out cakes with hands. Bake in medium oven.

Old-Fashioned Tea Cakes

1 cup sugar
2 eggs
½ cup of butter

Add vanilla flavoring. Add flour until stiff enough to roll out and bake.

Mrs. Zack Crittenden

Tea Cakes

Mix eggs, sugar, shortening and some flavoring together and bake.

Sue Peacock

Tea Cakes

2 eggs
2 cups sugar
¾ cup buttermilk
¾ cup butter (melted)

1 teaspoon vanilla
½ teaspoon baking soda
1½ teaspoon baking powder
plain flour

In a bowl beat the eggs well, and add sugar. Beat until mixed good. Add buttermilk, butter, vanilla, and soda and baking powder. Sift about six or eight cups flour into large bowl or broad tray. Make well in center and pour in the mixture, mixing with spoon until dough can be kneaded with the hands. Work in flour until stiff enough to handle. Roll out on floured board, and cut in size you want.

Mrs. Maye Price

Tea Cakes

1 cup sugar
1 cup butter
3 eggs

1 tsp. nutmeg
3½ cups flour

Lorenza Rhodes

Tea Cakes

Take a lump of lard. Put in sugar, I don't know how much, I just put it in. Mix an egg up in it. Mix little flour—enough to make it start rolling out. If you want you can lay pecans or raisins on it.

Irene Grisset

Old-Fashioned Tea Cake

6 eggs, leaving out 4 whites
2 cups sugar
½ cup butter

1 teaspoon soda, dissolved in
1 tablespoon vinegar

Cream butter and sugar.
Add eggs, one at a time.
Add soda mixture.
Add enough plain flour to make a soft dough, adding 1 teaspoon
   nutmeg to flour.
Roll thin, cut in rounds.
Place on a greased pan.
Bake in moderate oven until light brown.

Louise Jolly

Syrup Tea Cake

1 cup syrup
½ cup of cooking oil
4 tbs. of boiling water

1 teaspoon of ginger
⅓ tsp. flour

Mix all this together, roll out and put in a tray.

Mrs. Pauline Terry

Molasses Cookies

2 cups dark syrup
1 cup white sugar
1 cup melted butter or drippings,
   melted together
1 cup milk, sour

2 eggs
2 level teaspoons of soda
1 teaspoon of salt
1 rounded teaspoon of ginger
1 teaspoon cinnamon

Beat the shortening with the sugar; and the molasses and spices. Then
the beaten eggs. Put the soda in the sour milk. Add enough flour to
make a batter.

Mrs. J. H. Hankins

Ling Tartlets

1 lb. butter
½ lb. sugar
¾ lb. pounded almonds

1 lb. flour
½ lemon (grated)
1 tsp. powdered cinnamon

Beat butter to froth, beat in sugar, add the almonds, the grated half lemon, spice and flour. Stir well, make into little round balls the size of a walnut. Press these balls into little round tins. Make a hole in center and fill with currant jam. Roll some of the dough to make it look like a thick cord. Curl this on the top of each jam filling. Brush with beaten egg yolks and bake quickly.

Mrs. J. H. Hankins

Ginger Bread*

Mix a tablespoonful of ginger, a pinch of salt and a tiny pinch of soda; add 1 cupful of molasses (homemade) and a cup and a half of brown sugar if you can get it. Mix all of this together with flour as if making a hocake and you put it in the oven to bake. Test to see if it is done by sticking it with a broom straw—if no sticky looking cake is on the straw, it is ready.

Maggie Hart

Lafayette Ginger Bread

Cut up in a pan, ½ cup of fresh butter with ½ cup of brown sugar. Beat to a cream with a paddle. Add 1 cup West India molasses; 1 heaping teaspoon ground cinnamon, mace and nutmeg. Mix with 1 wine-glass of brandy. Beat 3 eggs until light and thick. Three cups of flour stirred in alternately. Mix in juice and grated rind of 1 large orange. Dissolve 1 teaspoon soda in warm water and stir in. Beat until very light. Bake in a loaf sheet in moderate oven.

Note: Ginger Bread came to America with the English and European settlers, and it is still much loved, though the ready mix variety we eat today is more cake than shortbread. Like the tea cake, it is pretty much an everyday affair. Our familiarity with it takes on legendary qualities—the gingerbread house of Hansel and Gretel and the gingerbread boy of the fairytale—and stuffed gingerbread boy and girl toys are quite often given to infants and children. Other contributors of gingerbread recipes not included here are: Mrs. J. T. Benson, Sr., Mattie Low Goodson, and Mrs. John Woodham.

Ginger Bread

1 cup of molasses
1 pinch of soda
½ cup of buttermilk

½ cup of butter
1 pinch of ginger
2 eggs

Mix all together in big bread tray-like biscuit dough and roll out on a floured board. Cut in squares with a knife.
    Bake in a biscuit baker until brown.

Mrs. Otis Walker

Burnt-Carmel Cake

1 cup of butter
2 cups of sugar
3 cups of flour
4 teaspoons of baking powder

1 cup of milk
1 teaspoon of flavoring
5 eggs

Sift dry ingredients together. Cream butter and sugar. Add eggs one at a time. Add milk alternately, with dry ingredients. Add flavoring last. Cook in 3 layers.

Filling

Put 2 cups of sugar and one cup of milk in boiler. Cook until a little thick. Put 1 cup of sugar in iron fryer. Melt over low heat. Put sugar and milk mixture into melted browned sugar. Cook a little, then spread on layers of cake.

Mrs. Maye Price

Lemon Cheese

Batter

½ cup shortening	½ t. salt
1 cup sugar	⅔ cup sweet milk
2 cups flour	2 t. vanilla
3 t. baking powder	3 egg whites

Mix as you would for a yellow cake, by creaming shortening & sugar. Add flour, salt & baking powder alternately with milk, and vanilla flavor and beaten egg white. Bake about 25 to 30 minutes in 350 degree oven or until springy.

Filling

4 t. butter	1 cup sugar
3 egg yolks	¼ t. salt
1 T. flour	juice of 2 lemons

Cook in double boiler until a thickness to spread.

Mildred Whatley

Chocolate Cake

1-2-3-4-Cake Layer

1 C shortening	1 C milk
2 C sugar	3 teaspoon baking powder
3 C flour	dash salt
4 eggs	

Cook in layers to suit yourself as to thickness; will make 5 nice layers. Cook 375 degree about 25 minutes or springy to touch.

Icing

½ cup butter	¼ C. light c. syrup
2½ C. sugar	3 T. cocoa or as dark as you want.
1 C. milk	dash salt

Bring to boil and cook on slow heat about 6 minutes spread over layers and side of cakes.

Mildred Whatley

Coconut Cake

Cake

1 c. butter	2¾ c. cake flour
2 c. sugar	1 c. buttermilk
5 eggs	1 t. vanilla
1 t. soda & dash salt	½ t. c. nut flavor

Cream butter, sugar, add eggs beating well after each addition; sift dry ingredients together, add to creamed mixture alternately with buttermilk. Stir in vanilla & c. nut flavoring. Bake in 3 or 4 greased & floured layer cake pans at 350 degrees for about 25 minutes.

Frosting

2 c. fresh coconut	C. nut milk or
½ st, oleo	½ c. sweet milk
2 c. sugar	

Cook until sugar is melted good—then spread between layers.

Mildred Whatley

Caramel Icing

3 c. sugar	½ c. butter
1 c. e. milk	1 t. vanilla

Cook the sugar and cream over low heat stirring until sugar is dissolved, cook until a small amount forms a soft ball when tried in cold water. Remove from fire, add vanilla. Beat until creamy enough to spread. Use 1-2-3-4 layer recipe or a white layer recipe.

Mildred Whatley

Carmel Cake

1½ cups sugar	4 or 5 eggs
2 cups flour	Stick of butter

Pour in flavoring and stir it in. Stir cake up and bake it.

Melt butter and put sugar and flavoring in and cook it thick; pour in milk. Makes a good filling.

Mrs. George Holliday

Cornmeal Sweet Cake

2 eggs   1 cup milk
1½ cups syrup   2 cups meal
½ cup butter

Frankie McCarty

Raised Flannel Cakes

Warm a quart of milk, put in a tablespoon of butter, add a little salt and two beaten eggs; stir in flour until the mixture is a thin batter. Add half a teacup of yeast; beat ingredients well. Set them overnight, if for breakfast, at noon, or for tea. Bake on a hot griddle.

Mrs. Weida Daughtery

Geranium Cake

Cream ½ teacup of butter with 1 cupful of pulverized sugar. Add, gradually, ⅔ cupful of water and 2 rounded cupfuls of flour which have been sifted with 2 teaspoonfuls of baking soda or powder. Fold in the stiffly-beaten whites of three eggs. Line a square with writing paper, butter it and place on the bottom a layer of rose-geranium leaves. Pour the mixture over the leaves and bake.

The results will be a delightful flavor, similar to the odor of rose petals; the leaves pull off readily. Boil ⅓ of a cupful of water and one teacupful of sugar until it rises, then add 3 tablespoonfuls of sweet cream and beat till cool; pour quickly over.

Mrs. Weida Daughtery

Wedding Cake

20 lbs. butter   1 oz. mace
20 lbs. sugar   4 oz. cinnamon
20 lbs. flour   20 glasses wine
40 lbs. currants   20 glasses brandy
20 nutmegs   10 eggs to the pound

Recipe used by Mrs. Ernst's Family

Wedding Cake

20 lbs. Butter
20 lbs. sugar
20 lbs. flour
20 glasses brandy
200 eggs
12 lbs. citron

40 lbs. currants
20 nutmegs
4 ounces cinnamon
1 mace
20 lbs. raisins

Serves 200 guests.

Mrs. Savannah Crenshaw

Jam Cake

5 eggs
2 cups sugar
1¼ cup butter
2 cups buttermilk
5 cups flour

1½ teaspoon soda
1 teaspoon salt
2 teaspoons cloves
4 teaspoons cinnamon
3 teaspoons cocoa

Cream butter, add sugar, which had been mixed with cocoa. Dissolve soda in buttermilk and add with flour and spices. Bake in a slow oven.

Mrs. George Yarbro

Raisin Cake

¾ cup of butter
2 cups of sugar
3 eggs (well beaten)
3 cups of flour
1½ cups of raisins-chopped
1 teaspoon of all-spices and cloves

1 cup of chopped nuts
1½ cup hot applesauce
1 round teaspoon of soda
1 teaspoon cinnamon
1 teaspoon nutmeg

Cook in layers and put together with any desired filling.

Mary Anne Wiley

Sally Lunn Cake

1 cup sugar
2 eggs
1 scant cup of milk
1 kitchen spoon of butter

1 teaspoon vanilla
2 cups flour
2 teaspoons baking soda or powder

Bake in a pan or cook in muffin rings.

Mrs. George McMurphy

Sally Lunn Cake

4 tbs. shortening   4 tbs. baking powder
4 tbs. sugar   1 egg
1 tbs. salt   ¾ cups milk
2 cups sifted flour

Stir shortening, salt and sugar together. Sift flour and baking powder
together. Add well-beaten egg to creamed mixture. Add flour and milk,
make a smooth batter. Bake in greased muffin pans or bread stick
molds. Bake in medium heated oven. Cook 25 minutes.

Mrs. Willis Wilson

Grandma Johnson's Devil's Food Cake

1 cup granulated sugar or 2 cups   ⅔ cups sour cream
    of brown sugar   ½ cup cocoa mixed with
Hunk of lard the size of an egg.   ⅔ cup hot water
2 beaten eggs   Pinch of salt
Mix the above   About two cups flour

Mix and bake until done.

Mrs. Sharon Thomas

Lane Cake

8 egg whites   3¼ cups flour
1 cup butter   2 teaspoons baking powder
1 cup milk   1 tablespoon vanilla
2 cups sugar

Sift the flour and baking powder together three times; cream butter
and sugar until light; then add alternatively, milk and flour. Last, beat
in well-whipped egg whites and vanilla. Bake in four layers at 350
degrees for about 25 to 30 minutes.

Filling

8 egg yolks   1 cup grated coconut
1¼ cups granulated sugar   1 cup of cut-up candied cherries
½ cup butter   ⅓ cup whiskey or wine
1 cup chopped pecans   1 cup finely chopped seeded raisins

Mrs. Emmanette Hughes

Lane Cake

White Layers

8 egg whites
2 cups sugar sifted
3 cups flour sifted 3 times
2 teaspoons baking powder

1 cup sweet milk
½ teaspoon salt
2 sticks butter
1 teaspoon vanilla

Cream butter and sugar real good. Add sifted flour and milk by degrees. Then add stiffly beaten egg whites. Add flavoring. Stack with favorite filling recipe.

Mrs. A. L. Patterson

Orange Cake

You take 2 eggs, 2 cups of sugar, 1 cup of milk, butter, whatever I think of, up to a pound, and you just mix in flour till it gets as stiff as you want it, and then you cook it in the oven. You use the juice from the oranges for flavoring, make it strong as you like. Now, for the filling, take 2 cups of sugar, 2 cups of milk and cook it until it just will drip off your spoon. Take 2 oranges, you peel one and grind up the peeling, grind up the other one whole, pour it all in the sugar and milk mixture and keep beating until it'll kind of thicken. Then put it on your cake when it gets done. It's a Christmas cake.

Mrs. Mary Will Glass

Japanese Fruit Cake

6 eggs
1 pound sugar
½ pound butter
1 pound flour

1 cup sweet milk
1 teaspoons yeast powders
1 teaspoon lemon extract

Divide batter in half. Bake two layers of the plain batter. In the other half put one cup seeded raisins, one tablespoon of ground spice, one teaspoon ground cloves, one teaspoon cinnamon. Bake in two layers also. Put layers together with the following:

One coconut grated, juice of two lemons, two cups sugar, one cup boiling water. Boil all together untill thick like starch. When cool, spice and put between layers.

Mrs. Mary Americus Williamson
(Muddie Wishy)

Fruit Cake

I can't give you an exact recipe. I just make it like Mama did. You start off with a pound cake: pound of sugar, pound of butter, pound of flour, pound of eggs, 10 or 12. And then you put whatever you've got or can afford in it—Mama didn't care for citron or orange peel, said it was tough to chew. I use a good many raisins, box of white and a box of dark, though some folks don't like so many. And then your pecans, however many you want, I like a lot, and your candied fruit, dredge all that good in flour and dump it in your batter. You have to use a big dishpan or something to hold it. And your spices, which ever ones you like, allspice, cinnamon, and nutmeg, put that in your batter before you stir in the fruit. If you want, you can add a cup of whiskey or wine, or even cold coffee. And I always put in some preserves, a pint of figs, peaches, strawberries, preserves make it moist. Then cook it in loaf pans or tube pans at a low heat. Set a little pan of water in the oven while you're cooking the cakes. It'll take half a day and night to cook it all. Now, it's good hot, but best after the flavors have all blended and settled; wrap it in a clean cloth; some folks put an apple in with it or dampen it every so often with whiskey; it'll keep a long time.

Mildred Whatley

Layer Cakes with Fillings

I always use the same recipe for all my stack cakes. Whatever the filling. It's that old 1, 2, 3, 4 recipe: 1 cup butter, 1 cup sweet milk, 2 cups sugar, 3 cups flour, 4 eggs, your soda, salt, and baking powder and vanilla flavoring. Cream the sugar and butter, add the eggs, beat after each one, alternate the flour mixture with the milk. It makes a right big cake, and I cook it in several thin layers and use a lot of filling.

Mildred Whatley

Lemon Cheese Cake

Cake

1 cup butter
2 cups sugar
1 cup milk
3½ cups flour

2 teaspoons baking powder
3 beaten egg whites
1 teaspoon vanilla

Thoroughly cream butter and sugar until light and fluffy; add sifted dry ingredients with milk, beating after each addition. Add vanilla. Fold in beaten egg whites. Bake in three pans. Bake in oven at 350 degrees.

Filling

8 egg yolks
1 cup sugar
½ scant cup butter

juice of 3 lemons
grated rind of 2 lemons

Beat egg yolks; beat in sugar and add butter. Cook in double boiler. When hot add lemon juice and rind. Stir constantly; when thick spread on cake while warm.

Mrs. Guy Wilson

Molasses Cake

1 egg
1 cup cooking oil
⅓ cup molasses
2 teaspoons ginger
2 teaspoons cinnamon
½ cup sugar

1 teaspoon soda
½ teaspoon soda
½ cup boiling water
2¼ cups flour
¾ cup raisins

Beat the egg, stir in the molasses, sugar and the boiling water. Sift the ingredients together. Add the first mixture, reserving ½ cup of flour to mix the raisins with. Stir in the raisins and the oil. Bake for thirty-five minutes at 375 degrees.

Mrs. I. U. Moore

Pound Cake

1 cup butter   6 eggs
1¾ cups sugar   2 cups flour

Cream butter and sugar; add one egg at a time, beating well after each addition. Add small amount of flour at times and beat well. Pour into greased and floured pan, bake in oven until done.

Mrs. Margaret Webb

Pound Cake

2⅓ cups of butter   6 large eggs
2½ cups of sugar   3 cups flour
¼ cup of sweet milk   1 teaspoon of vanilla flavoring
¼ teaspoon of baking powder

Cream sugar and butter. Add eggs, one at a time. Add flour that has been sifted with the baking powder in it—a small amount, alternate with milk, flavoring last.

Mrs. Charles Pride

Pound Cake

10 eggs   3½ cups sugar
1 lb. of butter   4 cups flour

Cream butter and sugar in a large bowl. Add one egg at a time, beat after each egg. Add flour—about ½ at a time. Beat until fluffy. Bake in a moderate oven until done; about 1½ hours.

Mrs. S. J. King

Pound Cake

1 lb. of sugar   9 eggs, beaten separately
1 lb. of flour   (separate whites from yellows)
¾ lb. of butter

Fold in whites last. Flavor with lemon extract. Bake in tube cake pan one hour or longer.

Floy Parmer

Buttermilk Pound Cake

3 cups plain flour
1⅓ cups butter
2½ cups sugar
⅓ cup buttermilk

½ teaspoon soda (level)
Vanilla and lemon (equal)
6 large eggs

Butter at room temperature. Cream with sugar. Add eggs one at a time. Beat well. Sift flour and soda 3 times. Add buttermilk last.
   Bake at 300 degrees.

Mrs. Rozelle Coxwell

Pound Cake

1 pound butter
1 pound flour

1 pound eggs (a dozen)
1 pound sugar

Cream sugar and butter in a large dish pan until creamy. Beat with wooden spoon. Add one egg and handful of flour at a time and beat well between each time until all mixture is added. Cook slow for about two hours.

Mrs. M. H. Solomon

Ginger-Drop Cakes

3 whole eggs
1 cup lard or any grease
1 cup sugar
1 cup molasses

1 tablespoonful ginger
1 tablespoonful soda dissolved in
   one cup boiling water
5 cups of flour

Beat up with spoon. Drop 3 inches apart in greased pan. *These are good.*

Mrs. Ruth Herren

One-Egg Cake

1 cup butter
1½ cup sugar
3 cups flour
1 cup sweet milk

1 egg
1 teaspoon soda
2 teaspoons cream of tartar (in flour)

Mrs. J. R. Burnett, Jr.
through a letter to
Mrs. Mary Americus Williamson
(Muddie Wishy)

Chocolate Fudge

2 c. sugar   4 T. cocoa (or more)
⅔ c. milk   ½ cup butter
1 T. light syrup   1 T. vanilla
1 cup nuts

Combine all but nuts and vanilla in boiler. Cook over medium heat until mixture boils, will form a soft ball in cold water. Cool slightly, add vanilla and nuts, stirring well. Lay out on platter. When cold, cut in bite-sized pieces.

Peanut or Pecan Brittle

1 cup grandulated sugar   2 tsp. baking soda
½ cup white corn syrup   1 tbs. butter
½ cup water   1 cup shelled pecans or peanuts

Cook sugar, syrup and water in deep iron skillet until a soft ball is formed when syrup is dropped in a cup of cold water.

Add nuts and continue cooking until the syrup is very brittle—or at crackling stage—when tested in cold water.

Remove from heat and add butter and soda. Stir until well mixed and foamy. Pour onto buttered cookie sheet and start pulling over wax paper while still hot. Cool just enough to handle and work fast.

Break large pieces of brittle and store in air-tight container and it will remain fresh and brittle for several days.

Mrs. Pearl Clark

Syrup Candy

2 cups syrup
1 lump of butter (the size of a walnut)

Boil these together until the mixture threads when you pour some from a spoon. Add ½ teaspoon soda and stir. After it quits foaming, pour out on a greased table top or platter. When it cools, pick up a little and begin to pull it. Keep adding a little more to what you have pulled until you have pulled it all. (To pull means to stretch it out then fold it back and stretch it again).

Mrs. Pearl Clark

Divinity

3 cups sugar
⅔ cups white corn syrup
Pinch of salt

Let boil until foams hard drops in water or threads from spoons. Pour slowly into thoroughly beaten whites of two or three eggs. Add one or two cups of nuts and beat until it thickens all.

Mrs. A. L. Patterson

Other Desserts

Pies, puddings, and custards are favorite Alabama desserts for everyday and Sunday dinner. The log tables of all-day singing and dinner-on-the-ground were (and are) always crowded with these sweets, and as the folks went down the line, they looked for Mrs. So and So's pecan pie or egg custard, since certain ladies were usually famous in the community for a particular dish. Our collectors found numerous recipes for buttermilk pie, egg custard, syrup custard, sweet-potato pie, pudding and custard and biscuit pudding (only a sampling of representative recipes have been included), which is among the most popular of this sort of dessert except for fruit pies, both plate and deep-dish or cobbler, which, naturally, appeared in the summertime. Sweet-potato custard, pecan pie, and syrup pies were autumn and winter dishes.

Nowadays, with the triumph of frozen foods, fruits are available year around, and so are the pies themselves—instant, complete, just thaw and serve, or thaw and heat; but fifty years ago, a fellow could "just taste" a fresh peach cobbler in the middle of January, longing for the real thing in July. Dewberries are the first fruits to ripen in Alabama, from late April to mid-May, and they usually serve for the first summer pie. After that, it's blackberries, peaches, apples, huckleberries, and, when frost falls, pumpkin, persimmon, sweet potato, and pecan. Rice and biscuit pudding and egg custards were served year 'round, though more often in winter. Chocolate, lemon, and coconut pies and puddings appeared less often on the table, since coconut and chocolate were luxury items not always readily available. Lemon, of course, was used quite often in extract form to flavor pies, cakes, puddings, and cream sauces.

For a cook, the beauty of a pie is that it can be made of whatever she happens to have in her pantry or stove: leftover rice, biscuit, or buttermilk, a bit of flour and sugar, some eggs and butter, or baked sweet potatoes, or some fresh fruit. In a real sense, these recipes are folk recipes—the folk always "make do" with what they've got.

Other favorite Alabama desserts include homemade ice cream (combined with various fresh fruits, especially peaches and dewberries, and sometimes even with violets!), ambrosia (usually made of oranges and coconut and served at Christmas time, though some cooks add apples, pineapple, nuts, and raisins), brandied fruits, and syllabub, a rich wine-and-milk beverage.

Pastry

2 cups flour
¾ tsp. salt

6 to 8 tbsp. shortening
6 to 8 tbsp. water

Cut in shortening with fork until about size of peas. Add water; dough will come away clean from sides of bowl. Roll out on floured cloth or table. Makes two shells or one large bottom and strips for lattice top.

Mrs. M. H. Solomon

Pastry Shells

10 tbs. of cold water
11 tbs. of shortening

½ tsp. salt
Enough flour to make dough roll out

Smooth enough for 3 (8 inch) pie plates

Mrs. Bert Hattaway

Apple Custard Pie

2 cups of stewed apples
4 eggs

3 cups of milk
Dash of cinnamon

Mix yolks of four eggs with three cups of milk; then mix in the apples thoroughly. Flavor with a dash of cinnamon. Finally, beat whites of four eggs and fold in. Filling should be put in a baked crust. Bake until firm.

Delicious Apple Pie

Filling

3 medium large apples	½ cup butter
1 cup sugar	1 tsp. vanilla

Pastry

2 heaping tablespoons shortening	Enough flour to form right
¼ cup cold water	consistency to roll
¼ tsp. salt	

Line pie plate with pastry. Peel and core apples and slice thin to fill the pie plate. Sprinkle sugar over the slices. Cut ⅔ of the butter over the apple slices, then drop the flavoring over them. Cover with the top crust and dot the remaining butter on top and bake for 25 to 30 min.

Mrs. Guy Wilson

Persimmon Pie

3 Large ripe cultivated persimmons	2 tablespoons butter
½ cup sugar	1 teasponon vanilla
2 eggs	

Peel and run through a potato ricer or sieve the fully ripe persimmons. Add the sugar, eggs, butter and vanilla.

   Put mixture in an uncooked pie shell and bake in moderate oven until set.

Lorene Peters, given to Louise Jolly

Mince Pies

Puff paste—use mincemeat. Roll out the puff paste to the thickness of a quarter of an inch, line some good-sized patty-pans with it. Fill them with mincemeat; cover with some paste and cut it close round the edge of the patty-pan. Put them in a brick oven. Beat the white of an egg stiff, froth, brush it over them when they are baked, sift a little powdered sugar over them—place them in the oven for a few minutes to dry the eggs.

   Serve them on a table napkin very hot. Cold mince pies will re-warm and be as good as fresh.

Mrs. Claude Smith

Pumpkin Pie

1½ cups cooked sifted pumpkin   ½ tsp. salt
½ cup brown sugar   1 tsp. cinnamon
2 cups milk   ¼ tsp. ground ginger
2 eggs

Add to the prepared pumpkin the sugar, salt, ginger, milk and eggs, beaten together. Then put into a pie plate that has been lined with pastry and baked in moderate oven until the filling is firm—about 35 minutes.

Miss Willie Dismukes

Pumpkin Pie

Press 1 qt. of cooked pumpkin through a sieve; beat yolks and whites of 9 eggs separately; mix together with 2 qts. of milk; stir in 1 tsp. each of mace, cinnamon, and ground nutmeg and 1½ cups of light brown sugar and a tbs. of brandy. Bake in an open crust until firm. This is a real old-fashioned pumpkin pie.

Sweet Potato Pie

2 or 3 medium size potatoes   Butter
Sugar   Spices

Take two or three medium size potatoes, peel, slice and boil until almost done. Place a layer of potatoes in an 8 inch pan. Slightly cover with sugar, dot with butter and add spices. Cover with a layer of dumplings. Add another layer of potatoes, butter, sugar, and spice. Add water then crust and bake.
    Make a regular pie pastry for the dumplings and crust.
    Approximately 1½ cups of sugar is needed.

Mrs. Eliza Dyess

Vinegar Pie

2 cups boiling water   3 eggs
¼ cup vinegar   1 tsp. lemon flavoring
1 cup sugar   ⅓ tsp. salt
2 tbs. flour   3 tbs. sugar

Mattie Hines

Butterscotch Pudding

1 quart and 1 half cup milk	2 eggs
5 spoons of flour	Hunk of butter
Cup of brown sugar	Vanilla
Pinch of salt	

Heat milk to boiling point and mix flour, sugar, and salt. Add dry ingredients to milk stirring all the while. Cool till thick, add beaten eggs and stir. Add butter and vanilla.

Mrs. Sharon Thomas

Sliced Potato Pie

Slice 3 or 4 sweet potatoes and boil a few minutes. Then have your dumplings dough ready.

Put a layer of potatoes then a layer of dumplings which has been rolled thin and cut in small pieces. Then put another layer of potatoes and a layer of dumplings. Pour a little syrup in this to make it as sweet as you like it. Put butter on top of dumplings. Bake until a golden brown.

Dumplings

About 1 cup of milk (buttermilk)	Lump of lard
Pinch of salt	Enough flour to make a stiff
½ tsp. soda	dough. Roll and cut.

Mrs. Joe McNeill

Sweet 'Tater Custard Pie

1 cup cooked, diced sweet potatoes	1 tbs. sifted flour
⅓ cup of butter, melted	Dash of salt
1 or 2 beaten eggs (if one egg	Nutmeg to taste
is used, add a little milk)	Pastry shell

Mix ingredients in the order given, pour into raw pastry pie shell and place in oven to bake. Bake until custard is set, in moderate oven.

Mrs. J. C. Howard

Berry Pudding

2 cups berries (black or
  huckle berries)
1½ cup of cornmeal
¼ cup of lard, or butter

1 tsp. salt
2 cups of water (more if needed)
Sweeten to taste with sugar
  or homemade syrup

Wash berries. Put in a heavy iron fryer; add fat, salt, water, and sugar or syrup which ever used. Heat to boiling and add a small amount of the cornmeal at the time; stir continually till all the meal is used. Stir occasionally to keep from burning; cook at least 30 minutes on top of stove.

Lillie G. McLellan

Blackberry Mush Pudding

1 cup syrup
1½ cup meal
4 or 5 tbs. of melted butter
1 egg

¼ cup buttermilk
Pinch of spice
Dash of salt
1½ pt. of blackberries

Mix in batter and stir in the berries. Bake in an iron frying pan.

Mrs. J. C. Hudson

Fruit Pie

Cook berries or fruit in a little water. Make dumplings out of cornmeal if flour not available. Add dumplings to cooked berries or fruit and put a crust on top. Make a sauce out of honey and milk and use in place of sugar.

Mrs. Amanda Hornsby

Green Tomato Pie

Lay in crust and sprinkle with a little flour. Slice fresh green tomatoes thinly and fill. Put in a level cup of sugar and half cup of butter; a dash of cinnamon or nutmeg. Pour 2 tbs. of vinegar over filling before putting on top crust. Bake in a moderate oven for a half hour. Serve hot.

Rose Reynolds

Gooseberry Pie

Wash the gooseberries and roll them in a tea towel to break off the little spines. Stew well in a small amount of water and add generous quantity of sugar (enough to sweeten to taste.) Roll out-cover dough thin, pinch into lower crust and cut "di-does" in top. Bake in moderate oven.

Rose Reynolds

Ice [Irish] 'Tater Pie

Peel 'tater
Slice round or cut 'em long—let 'em boil 'til they get soft.
Use a pie pan. Add as much as you would like of sweet milk. Lay little slices in milk, then add butter and yo' salt and pepper.
Roll ya some flour dough lik' a crust
Slice like 'ghettie [spaghetti]. Crisscross over 'taters. Add 'nother layer of 'taters over that. Take another piece of dough, roll it out wide and place it on top of pan.
Let bake long enough to cook crust

Rose Reynolds

Biscuit Puddin'

Ingredients:

1. Cold Biscuits
2. Sugar
3. Sweet Milk
4. Eggs
5. Butter
6. Flavoring

Crumble the biscuits up and soak soft with sweet milk. Add eggs, sugar, melted butter, and flavoring. Stir it all together, pour into a pan and place it in a stove and cook.

Luna Roberts

Biscuit Pudding

Crumbling biscuits, soak them in sweet milk, add sugar and butter, beat up orange or lemon peel, add yellow of eggs and make meringue out of whites of eggs.

Ruth Tye

Biscuit Pudding

Put yo' left-over biscuits in milk. Place them in a pan. Add a pinch of salt and an egg. Add baking powder 'cording to how much you goin' to make. Then put yo' butter in it.

You can use flavor or spice but I like spice, nutmeg spice. Put this in a pan and bake it. Let rise and bake like a cake.

Rose Reynolds

Old-Fashioned Biscuit Pudding

5 cold biscuits	¼ tsp. allspice
1 cup sugar	¼ lb. butter
1½ cups syrup	4 eggs
½ tsp. cinnamon	1¾ cup milk (sweet)

Crumble biscuits, pour milk over and let stand ½ hr. Add eggs and the rest of ingredients and bake one hour.

Mrs. Lewis Williams

Egg Custard

Use glass for measuring. Break three eggs in glass. Hold back the whites of two for meringue. Hold your thumb on glass and use twice as much sugar by measure and three times as much milk. Add a dash of nutmeg. Pour into unbaked pie shell and bake until done.

Egg Custard

4 eggs	⅔ cups sugar
½ tsp. salt	¼ tsp. nutmeg
2⅔ cups scalding milk	1 tsp. vanilla

Louise Weeks

Egg Custard

4 eggs	butter
1 cup sugar	2 cups milk
1 heaping tablespoon flour	

Laura Turner

Three-Egg Custard Pies

9 eggs (use whites of two eggs)   4 cups milk
2 cups sugar   ¾ cup butter
3 tsp. vanilla   3 tbs. butter

Mix all ingredients together and bake in three pastry shells.

Mrs. Mabel Dozier

Syrup Custard

4 eggs   ½ cup of sugar
1 cup of syrup   2 tbs. of butter

Pour in baked 9-inch pastry shells. Bake in hot oven.

Mrs. E. R. Mack

Syrup Custard

3 eggs   1½ cups milk
¼ lb. butter   1 cup sugar-cane syrup

Beat eggs slightly, add milk, butter and syrup. Pour into a pastry-lined pie plate and bake in a hot oven (250 to 300 degrees for 10 minutes). Reduce heat and bake 30 to 40 minutes or until filling is firm.

Mrs. Ira Griswold

Syrup Custard

3 eggs   1 cup of sugar
1 cup of red syrup   3 dabs of butter

Jackie Kinsauld

Syrup and Egg Pie

2 cups sugar cane syrup   Unbaked 9-inch pie shell
4 eggs   2 tbs. cornstarch

Heat syrup but do not boil. Beat eggs thoroughly. Pour them slowly into syrup, stirring constantly. Mix cornstarch in two tablespoons of the mixture and stir. Bring to a boil, stirring until it begans to thicken. Pour into unbaked pie shell and bake at 325 degrees until firm.

Mrs. Emmanette Hughes

Buttermilk Pie

3 eggs
1 cup sugar
2 tbs. flour

¼ cup melted butter
1 cup buttermilk
1 tsp. vanilla or lemon flavoring

Beat eggs slightly and add sugar and flour. Then add melted butter and mix well. Add buttermilk and flavoring and pour into unbaked pie shell. Bake at 325 degrees F. until custard is set.

Mrs. Martin Griswold
Mrs. Florine Metcalf

Buttermilk Pie

2 cups buttermilk
3 eggs
1½ cups sugar
½ cup soft butter

4 tbs. flour
1 tsp. vanilla
2 uncooked pie crusts

Cream butter, sugar and egg yolks. Add flour and mix good. Add buttermilk and stir. Add beaten egg whites. Pour in crusts.

Mrs. Susie Jackson

Grated Sweet Potato Pudding

Grate 2 medium sweet potatoes (raw). Add 3 well-beaten eggs, 1 cup sweet milk, 1 cup sugar, 2 tablespoons cane syrup, 1 teaspoon (level) salt. Melted butter the size of an egg. Add a dash of nutmeg and cinnamon.
   Mix well and bake until firm and light brown. Serve with any pudding sauce, if desired.

Louise Jolly

Grated Sweet 'Tater Puddin'

Peel sweet taters and grate them raw (about two cups). Add a cup of syrup, two eggs, a dab of spice, and a little more than a dab of fried meat grease and a pinch of salt. Put it in a pan and bake in the oven.

Mrs. Margie White

Potato Pudding

Grate 5 cups raw sweet potatoes. Add 1 cup can syrup, 1 cup brown sugar, ½ cup butter, 3 eggs, ⅓ cup flour, and 1 tsp. allspice. Mix and bake.

Mary Olive Byrd

Sweet 'Tater Puddin'

Boil 'taters 'til soft.
Drain yo' water off of it.
Add stick of butter to 'taters . . .
A little salt, and
'bout half a teaspoon full of baking powder.
Mash 'taters up. Add an egg to it. Put it in pan. Put it in the stove and bake 'till stiff and brown.

Rose Reynolds

Grated Sweet Potato Pudding*

Peel three or four large sweet potatoes and grate. Mix cup of sugar, ½ cup of sweet milk, 2 eggs, 1 tsp. allspice, 1 tsp. cinnamon, 1 tsp. vanilla. Bake slow until done.

    Wood Stove—3 sticks wood = fast cooking
                 2 sticks wood = medium cooking
                 1 stick wood = slow cooking

Mrs. M. H. Solomon

*Other recipes for grated sweet potato pudding, not included here because they were all substantially the same, were contributed by Mary Hammack, Miss Callie Ward, and Mrs. Susie Jackson.

Indian Puddin'

5 cups milk   1 teaspoon salt
⅓ cup corn meal   1 teaspoon ginger
½ cup molasses

Scald 4 cups of the milk and add corn meal slowly. Cook in double boiler about 20 minutes. Add molasses, butter, salt, and ginger. Pour into baking dish that has been buttered and pour on the cup of cold milk. Set dish in pan of hot water and bake 2 hours in a slow oven.

Mrs. Susie Jackson

Old-Fashioned Molasses Pudding

1 egg
⅔ cup molasses
3 tablespoons shortening melted
1 teaspoon vanilla extract
½ cup chopped raisins
½ cup chopped nuts

1¾ cups sifted all-purpose flour
½ teaspoon soda
1 teaspoon baking powder
½ teaspoon salt
1 teaspoon cinnamon
½ cup water

Louise Weeks

Peach or Apple Tarts

Cook dried apples or peaches in a little water until tender, cooking all water. Mash up with fork. Add sugar to taste. Roll out pastry as if for pie, only a bit less shortening, or you can use self-rising flour and roll out thin. Cut circles with saucer. Lay on cooked fruit down the middle of circle. Fold over. Prick edges together with fork, be sure to seal tight. Fry in deep fat, turning once, until brown. Or you can bake in oven, brushing with butter, and when, a little cool, sprinkling with sugar and cinnamon.

Mrs. Mackie Pienezza

Poor-Man's Pudding

Meal
Syrup
Eggs

Buttermilk (with soda)
Butter
Flavoring (orange peel)

Bake in moderate oven until done.

Mrs. A. B. Gantt

Popcorn Pudding

Three pints each of sweet milk and popcorn, every kernel popped white and not a bit scorched, two beaten eggs, one-half teaspoonful of salt, mix all together and bake one-half hour. Serve with sweetened cream or milk.

Sidney Taylor

Rice Pudding

½ cup of uncooked rice
  [most recipes, however,
  specify left-over cooked rice]
4 cups of milk scalded

Dab of salt
¼ cup of sugar
2 dabs of butter

Louzina Rhodes

Meringue Rice Pudding

1 cup cooked rice (cold is best)
3 oz. butter
3 egg yolks

1 teaspoon vanilla
2 cups sweet milk
1 cup sugar

Add sugar to cold rice. Add 3 egg yolks and mix well. Add butter, vanilla and milk. Blend well and pour into greased baking dish. Put in moderate oven and bake until moisture is absorbed, but not too dry. Cool.

Beat egg whites to which a pinch of salt has been added. Add 6 tablespoons sugar, one at a time and beat until stiff. Spread meringue on the pudding and put in hot oven until meringue is light brown.

Lucille Lightfoot

Peach-and-Berry Cobbler

Roll out enough pastry to make bottom and top, plus some for dumplings. Wash fruit, cook up in boiler until tender, add sugar to taste, it'll take a good bit.

Line a deep skillet or pan with pastry. Pour in fruit, add dots of butter, as much as you want. Some folks sprinkle nutmeg or cinnamon on peaches, it's good with or without. Pinch off dough in little balls, poke into fruit, cover with top crust or strips and lattices. Put a little butter on crust. Bake in fairly hot oven till crust browns and juice bubbles up around sides.

Mrs. M. H. Solomon

Pecan Pie

1 cup corn syrup	pinch of salt
½ cup sugar (brown or white)	1 t. vanilla
3 eggs	1 cup pecans
2 T. butter	

Beat eggs, add sugar, syrup, melted butter, and rest of ingredients. Pour in uncooked pastry shell. Bake in slow oven for about 45 minutes, or until knife comes out clean.

Mrs. Ruth Herren

Lemon Pie

¾ c. sugar	3 T. lemon juice
1 c. scalded milk	1 grated lemon rind
3 T. corn starch	1 t. butter
3 eggs	⅛ t. salt

Mix cornstarch, sugar & salt. Add the hot liquid stirring constantly. Cook in a double boiler—until mixture is thick. Separate eggs and beat yolks slightly. Slowly add them to the hot liquid and the flavoring. Continue cooking until mixture is thick. Cool, slightly, pour into a baked pastry shell. Cover with meringue, bake in a slow oven.

Mildred Whatley

Chocolate Pie

½ c. sugar	4 T. cocoa
2 c. hot milk	⅛ t. salt
4 T. corn starch or flour	1 t. vanilla
3 eggs	

Mix cornstarch, sugar and salt. Add the hot milk, stirring constantly. Cook in a double boiler until mixture is thick, continuing to stir. Separate eggs, beat yolks slightly. Slowly add them to the hot liquid and chocolate, continue cooking until mixture is thick. Cool slightly, add vanilla, pour into a baked pastry shell, cover with meringue made from the whites of the egg. Bake in a slow oven (250 degree to 300 degree) until a delicate brown.

Mildred Whatley

Grandmother Holland's Homemade Ice Cream

Use eggs you have on hand
2 or 3 double hands full of sugar
As much flour as you can pick up between the tips of your fingers.

Pick three or four peaches off tree, mash up with rolling pin. Put in the other mixture.
Put in freezer—Fill freezer with what sweet milk you have.
Ice (which came from Luverne) and put in a hole in the smoke house and cover with sawdust to freeze.

Merle Dansby

Vanilla Ice Cream

2 cups hot milk   2 eggs (separated)
2 tbs. flour or cornstarch   2 tsp. vanilla
1 cup sugar   1 qt. cream

Make a custard of the first four ingredients as follows: Mix flour or cornstarch, sugar and ⅛ tsp. salt, adding the milk gradually. Cook over hot water 10 minutes, stirring occasionally. Stir into the well-beaten eggs very gradually. Cook until the mixture coats the spoon. Cool, add cream, stiffly beaten egg whites and flavoring. Strain beaten egg whites and flavoring, strain and freeze in freezer as desired at first.

Charles Ferguson

Violet Ice Cream

1 qt. cream
¾ cup sugar
Few grains salt

⅓ cup yvette cordial
1 small bunch violets
Violet coloring

Mix first four ingredients. Remove stems from violets and pound violets in a mortar until well lacerated, then strain through cheese cloth—add extract to first mixture; color, freeze and mould. Serve garnished with fresh or candied violets; the light cultivated violets should be used and the result will be gratifying.

Mrs. Fred Foley

Brandied Peaches

1 peck peaches (skinned)
sugar to half their weight
1 qt. brandy

Alternate in stone jar, layer of peaches with sugar until filled. Add brandy. Cover closely, using cheese cloth or unbleached muslin under the jar cover. Can be used after one week. Keep in cool place.

Mrs. Cecil Colquitt

Brandied Peaches

Place in a crock churn alternate layers of peaches and sugar. Cover tightly, but don't seal. Bury in earth until Christmas eve. Unearth and enjoy.

Mrs. M. H. Solomon

Ambrosia

6 to 8 oranges (sliced into circles)
1 coconut (grated)
1 cup sugar

Arrange oranges in a layer and spread coconut and sugar nest. Add other layers until the bowl is full.

Mrs. L. G. Brown

Syallabub

1 qt. of rich milk
1 cup of wine
½ cup sugar

Put sugar and wine into a bowl and the milk (heated to lukewarm) in a separate bowl. When sugar is dissolved in wine, pour the milk in, holding it high, pour the mixture back and forth until it is frothy. Grate nutmeg over it.

Hattie Mae Mills

Country Syllabub

½ lb. white sugar
1 pint fine cider or white wine

Mix wine and sugar together. Grate nutmeg. Prepare mixture in a large bowl, just before milking time, then let it be taken to the cow and have about 3 pints milked in it, stirring it occasionally with a spoon. Let it be beaten and eaten before the froth subsides.

Mrs. L. R. Ernst

Tutti Frutti

1 cup brandy (the best you have)
1 cup sugar
1 cup ripe strawberries

Into a stone jar put the cup of brandy, the cup of sugar, and the cup of strawberries. Stir thoroughly. As each fruit comes to the height of its perfection in season, add it, with a cup of sugar for each cup of fruit. No more brandy is indicated. Be sure to stir at each addition. Large fruits like peaches should be cut into small pieces. Atop vanilla ice cream, this is a delight.

Note: Startings of this mixture are now given to friends and neighbors, who add a cup of fruit and a cup of sugar every two weeks.

Mrs. Cecil Colquitt

(((⊛ ⊅ ○ ⟨ ○ ⟨ ⊙ ⟨ ⊙ ⌒ ☺) ⅏) (((⊛ ⊅ ○ ⟨ ○ ⟨ ⊙ ⟨ ⊙ ⌒ ☺) ⅏) (((⊛ ⊅

Meats

The meat recipes in this collection reflect the inventiveness and thrift of the folk. Often compelled to do without domestic meat in hard times, they killed wild fowl and animals for food—partridges, rabbits, squirrel, possum, deer, and even owl, frogs, and terrapin; and every edible portion of the hog, down to its life blood, was consumed. Readers will wonder why there are so few beef recipes. The explanation lies, of course, in the fact that raising beef cattle for human consumption did not become a major industry in Alabama until the late '30s and early '40s; the conversion from cotton to beef was not complete until the '50s. There were exceptions. Mrs. Ruth Herren of Tallassee, Alabama, tells us that her father slaughtered no pork whatever on account of his religious beliefs: one must not eat that with cloven hoof, only that which "cheweth the cud." She recalled how Mr. Burton stored fresh beef in the cellar, dug a trench around it, and cooked it with well water. Of English descent, he had a great fondness for dried beef and was an expert at this method of preservation. Two other recipes point out the use of beef in nineteenth-century Alabama—ox tail soup and calf's head stew.

The principal sources of domestic meats were chicken and hogs. Both are of infinite variety in preparation. Hog-killing day was momentous and, as a matter of fact, hog-killing amounts to a folk craft or skill in its own right. *Foxfire* has published a step-by-step, photographically illustrated guide to hog slaughter, a tedious and lengthy process that begins with the initial death blow, delivered by a bullet or wooden club; continues with the bleeding, scalding, actual chopping, sawing, and cutting of portions; and ends with the lard rendering, sausage and souse making, salting down, and smoking.

Chicken killing was faster and simpler, and was usually done by the housewife herself. She captured the old stewing hen or spring chicken—either by deception, surprise, or strenuous chase—and wrung its neck swiftly and surely, or chopped it off with a hatchet at the chopping block; plucked its feathers (saved for a mattress); singed it; and finally dressed it for stewing, baking, or frying. A fat hen was usually boiled, the juices being drawn off for dressing, and the hen then baked. The tougher ones were boiled all day and went into soups and, along with a rabbit or some goat, into Brunswick or Camp Stew.

There is no such thing as Southern Fried Chicken—that is, no standard recipe, even in one state. Every cook has her own way of preparing it—some skin it, some don't; some coat the pieces with buttermilk, sweet milk, egg, or all three. Some fry it at a high temperature in deep fat, others at a medium heat with a moderate amount of grease. The best place to see and taste the varieties of fried chicken is a family reunion or an all-day-singing and dinner-on-the-ground. You can get a piece with hard, thick crust, its opposite, a thin crust, or something in between. And, as there are a variety of recipes, so is there a wide range of favorite pieces. Some folks prefer the drumstick, others the thigh or the wishbone, a few claim the liver, infants often teeth on the gizzard, and there is a select coterie of wing eaters. The people who don't like fried chicken are nearly as scarce as hen's teeth.

Small pigs and goats were roasted whole, larger ones in shanks, shoulders, and butts, over an open pit for barbecues. Hog meat from several hogs killed during the winter provided the bulk of the house-wife's cooking—some fresh tenderloin, ribs, and sausage were cooked immediately, the rest put up in jars. Even chitterlings and brains were preserved. Hams, middling meat, and fatback were salted, sugar cured, and smoked. A sixty-year-old man in Crenshaw County told us a hog-killing story last spring: "Fellow come after me one morning early. Said he wanted me to kill hogs for him. I got my gun and we went on over there. He had a hillside full of hogs. I said which one you want me to shoot. He thought on it a minute and said 'Tell you what, Shoot the first one what raises his head.' Directly a big old hog raised his head. I shot him. The fellow killing the hogs said 'Now, shoot the next one what raises his head,' and I did. 'Now, shoot the next one.' I did. It kept on like that a spell. I'd shoot and he'd say 'Now, the next one that raises his head.' Shot twenty hogs that day."

On that day we were watching Mr. Andrew Burgans weave-split white-oak baskets. In his prime Mr. Burgans was also a logger and a maker of wooden shingles. One story brought on another—tales of swamps, thickets, piney woods, recalcitrant mules, hunting, and the relative merits of, and various methods for, preparing possum, squir-rel, rabbit, and even coon. All agreed that you had to boil possum and coon to get the stink out and then bake them with sweet potatoes. All the men expressed fondness for partridges, frog legs, and eel, but it was some time later before we heard of blackbird stew. "Four and twenty blackbirds baked in a pie," says the nursery rime, and the poor startled king watches his dinner fly away singing. Mr. and Mrs. Joe Yates of Kent, Alabama, still cook blackbird stew—a dish fit for a king!

According to Mrs. Yates: "You take three or four birds and maybe a squirrel and boil in not too much water—'bout 'nuf to make 2 cups of liquor—'til the meat comes off the bone and you take the birds out and add salt and pepper and butter and you let this boil up and take your dumpling batter and roll it out as thin as paper and you cut it up in strips and drop four or five in the boiling liquor and take them out when they look done and add four or five more until you have cooked up all the dumplings. Then you add about a cup of sweet milk and let it all come to a good boil."

Good Fried Chicken

Kill and dress a chicken that will weigh about 3½ pounds. It will dress out about 2½ lbs. Salt it and let it set in the ice box about an hour before cooking. Put into a deep fryer in deep fat after thoroughly rolling in flour. Keep lid on tight, turning only once. Drain most of the fat away and make flour gravy (being careful to leave crumbs in pan). Smother for about ½ hour and serve with hot biscuits and other food. Very good to serve for breakfast when men have lots of heavy work.

Hen and Dressing

Get you a good sized stewing hen. Kill, pluck, singe, and clean it good. Put in large vessel with a good amount of water. Cover and cook on medium heat until fork sticks tender. If you haven't cooked it till the meat falls off the bones, you can stick in the oven and brown it. While hen is cooking, make up your dressing. Crumble up left-over cornbread and biscuit, even grits left from breakfast, into large bowl. Break 6 to a dozen eggs over it, depending on how much bread you've got. Pour over a right smart of chicken broth, add chipped onion, some celery, if you've got it, salt, pepper to taste. Mixture ought not be dry. Pour into skillet and bake in a pretty hot oven. If you want, you can add some of the chicken meat to the dressing. Serve with giblet gravy, made out of liver, gizzard, hard boiled eggs, all chipped up, some of the broth, and a little flour.

Mrs. M. H. Solomon

Chicken and Dumplings

"When I make biscuits for dinner, I save back some of the dough. I put my chicken on to boil, when it's done, I take out all the bones, roll out my dough thin, cut it in strips, then little blocks out of the strips and drop it in the chicken broth. If you want chicken pie, you just make pastry crust and put in the oven to bake. When the crust is brown, I always take it out and add some sweet milk to freshen it, set it back in the oven to heat real good. Mama used to make chicken pie in a great old big pan. Used to, people left the bones in the pie, the bony pieces especially, the wings, necks, and backs saved from the frying, but I pick my bones out now, these old chickens you get today, they don't even smell right, all bruised and bloody. I cut all that off."

Mrs. Ruth Herren

Ham Balls

Chop fine old ham, cooked, add one egg for each person to be served, with a little flour—according to the quantity of mixture you have— beat well, make into balls, fry in hot lard.

Sidney Taylor

Scrapple

4 lbs. pork (chop roast is best)	1 teaspoon pepper
1½ gal. water	white corn meal
3 teaspoons salt	1 tablespoon ground sage

Cook pork in the one and half gallons of water for 2 hr. Place on platter and shred with fork and small knife. Place back in water and add salt and pepper. Add white corn meal very slowly, stirring constantly, and when mixture is thick enough to "stand up," pour into pan to mold. When cool, place in refrigerator to chill. To serve, cut in ½-in. slices and fry in deep fat.

Chitterlings

Put in a lot of water—boil until tender—salt and pepper. Take out, cut in little giblets. Or size of stuffed sausage links, drain off water. Flour like any other meat and fry 'em.

Rose Reynolds

Pickled Pigs' Feet

Scrape and clean them thoroughly. Put in kettle and boil for four or five hours until soft. Add salt to taste during boiling. Take out and pack in a crock or stone jar. Boil vinegar and spice well; pour vinegar over pig feet until covered. Allow them to stand for several days before serving.

Liver Sausage

Grind up liver and sausage meat in equal amounts. Add: red pepper, black pepper, sage, and salt to suit your taste. Stuff this mixture in hog chitterlings. Then hang the sausage in the smokehouse and smoke it for two or three days with green oak or hickory.

Eunice Calloway

Liver Sausage

Cook liver, heart, melts, and lights until they are real tender, then grind in a food grinder. Season with salt, pepper, and sage, and stuff like any other sausage. Smoke until the casting rattles. They can be eat this way or can be warmed.

Mrs. Will Godwin

Hog Souse

Get a hog head and feet, clean it good singe both and scrape real clean, put in vessel large enough to cook well done and when it has cooked down and tender, remove from water, pick out all bones, mash up well with your hand. Add home-grown red pepper pods cut—black pepper, sage, salt, and vinegar to taste. Put in clean, white flour sack and hang up to drip, weight down with sad iron for two or three days in cold weather.

Mrs. M. H. Solomon

Hog's Head Cheese
(Souse)

Cook four hog's heads, feet, ears, and all. Boil these parts until they are tender. Remove all meat from the bones, add two teaspoons sage, two teaspoons ground red pepper, salt to taste, and mix well. Use a small bag, and press bag tightly to get all the juice out. Then let the bag hang and drip over night. It should be kept in a cool place. It can be sliced into pieces, or small chunks when it is firm like butter. Some like it this way but others pour hot vinegar over it.

Mrs. Fannie Bryan

Hog's Head Cheese

Cook 4 hog's heads, feet, ears, and all. Boil until tender. Pick meat off the bones. Add 2 tbs. ground sage, 2 tsp. ground red pepper. Salt to taste. Mix well. Put in 25-lb. flour bag. Press down in bag tightly. Hang and let drip over night. Keep in cool place or cut in chunks and pour hot vinegar over it and close tightly.

Mary Olive Byrd

Hog Souse

Get the head of a hog and cook it down. After it has cooked down, either grind or mash up the meat real fine. Add seasonings; salt, black and red pepper, vinegar or pepper sauce. Press for about twenty-four hours. Slice and eat.

Mrs. Margaret Crittenden

Souse

1 hog head
2 teaspoon sage
2 teaspoon salt

Cook hog head until it will fall off bone. Work it up real fine. Add salt and sage. Put in clean flour sack and press real tight until cold. Slice and serve.

Mrs. Martin Griswold

Liver Pudding

One pork liver
3 onions chopped fine
1 pint cracklins
1 tablespoons salt

Dash red pepper
Dash cayenne pepper
Dash of sage
1 teaspoon black pepper

Grind in food chopper and mix well. Press down over night in cool place.

Liver Pudding

Take a liver, lights, head, and feet from a hog and cook tender all through. Work together and season with salt, pepper, and sage. Cook together and thicken with corn meal.

Mrs. Emmie Prestwood

Blood Pudding

When you kill a hog and stick him in the neck, catch the blood. Put it on the stove and thicken it with flour. Season it with sage, pepper and salt. Bake in an oven.

Mrs. Emmie Prestwood

Blood Pudding

At hog-killing time, get your neighbors to save the blood for you. Mix enough meal with the blood to make it thick and season with salt and pepper. Bake.

Evelyn B. Dean

Recipe for Blood Pudding Sausage

When killing hogs, stick them in the heart with a knife; catch the blood
in a pan, cook some ground meat, and a large amount of rice; then add
the blood to make a soft paste; add parched red pepper, salt, garden
sage, and black pepper; cook on low heat till thick, then stuff the
sausage and put in the smoke house, and smoke until dry.

Mrs. J. M. Moore

Boiled Tongue

1 fresh tongue
5 cloves
6 peppercorns

1 tablespoon lemon juice
1 tablespoon vinegar
½ teaspoon salt

Eugene Brown

Terrapin Tongue With Blackberry Sauce

1 fresh beef tongue
1 glass blackberry jelly or jam
Cloves
1 or 2 (fresh) bay leaves
1 cupful raisins, cooked till
  tender in 1 cupful water

juice of 1 lemon
salt water
1 tablespoon mixed pickle spice
dried celery tips
salt

Cook tongue till very tender in salted water containing a tablespoon of
mixed pickle spice, one or two extra bay leaves, and a few dried celery
tips. When very tender, remove the skin, trim off the root end and stick
the solid meat full of cloves. Place in a greased baking pan, dust with
salt, pour over the jelly, beaten with a fork, add the lemon juice and
bake 20 minutes, basting with cooked raisins. Serve cold.

Mrs. Lewis Carroll

Ground Hog

To cook ground hog cut a big onion and place in water used to preboil
the meat. Preboil three times. Drain off water and onion, roll meat in
flour and fry.

Snow Bird

Stuff each bird with an oyster, place in a dish and add a little boiled pork, and oyster liquor, season well with butter, pepper and salt. Cover the dish with crust and bake in moderate oven.

Barbequed Eel

Take eel and place on hot fire and let eel cook until outside is crispy. Remove from fire and slice up in round slices. Ready to eat.

Todd Pierce

Smoked Sausage

8 lbs. lean pork with some fat	2 tablespoons black pepper
3 tablespoons salt	2 tablespoons sage—ground or rubbed

Measure and mix seasoning. Sprinkle over ground pork, mix thoroughly with hands. Can be ground the second time for a finer grade of sausage. Stuff in casings with sausage grinder stuffer. When they are stuffed, hang over about 3 inch hickory poles and put a smoke from green hickory chips under sausage to smoke two or three days. Poles should be at least 5 feet above smoker.

Mrs. George Moreman

Madrilene

Knuckle of veal	2 cloves stuck in a small parsnip
2 lbs. chopped round beef	1 stalk celery
1 large can tomatoes	1 laurel leaf
1 clove garlic	Small can beets
2 carrots	Parsley
1 small white turnip	Pepper
5 qts. cold water	2 teaspoons rock salt
2 leeks	

Peel and wash the soup vegetables and cut up in big pieces. Put the knuckle of veal to soak in the water for a half-hour. Add other ingredients. Heat slowly and let simmer for 5 or 6 hours, being careful to skim when necessary. Strain carefully through fine wet cheesecloth. Cook and remove grease. Color to pale red with beet juice and season to taste. May be served cold with slice of lemon, or hot with chopped parsley.

Backbone

Boil fresh backbone on top of stove until tender, then bake until crusty in oven. Or boil it awhile, then add your fresh greens, turnips, collards, mustard, or a mixture. Backbone is good to make soup, too. Open up a jar of tomatoes, jar of peas, butter beans, corn, beans, add some chopped onions and some white potatoes, put it all in an iron pot, add water and salt and pepper, cook slow till all is tender. Boil up your backbone and have it done first, though.

Spare Rib

At hog killing time, boil up ribs until tender. After boiling, can bake in hot oven till brown or fry in skillet on top of stove. Good with dry peas, turnips, collards, or for breakfast with syrup and biscuit.

Tenderloin

Cut in pieces a little smaller than your hand. Salt and pepper to taste. Put a little grease in bottom of skillet. Fry, turn often. Can add water to steam tender, then fry down again. Pour cup of coffee in grease for gravy.

Pork Shank or Butt and Dressing

Get you a good shank or butt. Put in deep kettle. Nearly cover with water. Set to boil, add salt and pepper, cook two or more hours until tender. Make dressing out of broth. Skim off some fat, depending on how greasy you want dressing. Work broth into left over cornbread and biscuit, add salt, pepper, sage, good bit of onion, eggs. Pour into iron skillet or baker. Cook until crust starts to form around edges. To bake; boil on top of stove an hour or so. Take out of water, put in deep skillet, bake in medium to slow oven till done. Can cover with a jelly or jam glaze and score with cloves, if you want, or, towards last hour of the cooking, lay on some peeled sweet potatoes and keep basting with juice.

Cured Ham

Rinse off mold, if any. Put in iron skillet or large baker. Stick cloves all over it. Bake in moderate oven until tender. Can make glaze, if desired, out of juice from fig preserves, any jams or jellies mixed with a little dried or bought mustard. Add glaze at the last of the cooking. Can also boil up cured ham like fresh pork. To fry: slice off several pieces from ham with sharp butcher knife. Put only a little grease in skillet. Fry, browning good but not till tough. Make gravy by adding some coffee or water.

Fried Partridges

Dress birds, clean real good. Cut up like chicken or in quarters. You can bake or fry them whole, if you want. Salt and pepper, dredge in flour. Fry in medium-hot grease until brown, add some water and simmer, will make a good gravy. Serve with biscuit, butter, and syrup.

Mrs. M. H. Solomon

How to Broil Rabbit or Squirrel

Dress and skin carefully. Cut off and throw away the head and feet. Cut in two pieces through the backbone. Place in roaster over coals until brown, turn and brown on other side. Sprinkle with salt and pepper, then cook slowly over coals, turning occasionally, until tender.

Fried Rabbit or Squirrel

Dress squirrel. Cut up like chicken. Salt and pepper. Flour it good. Put in skillet of hot grease, enough to half cover meat. Brown and turn until tender. Can add a little water and steam with lid on or lift out meat and make gravy. Add a handful or so of flour and a bit of milk or water, a bit more salt and pepper. Good with hot biscuits for breakfast or supper when it's cold weather.

Mary Will Glass

Squirrel Dumplings

2 old squirrels

Boil for two hours. Put a piece of fat pork (3 inches by 1 inch) when it starts to boil. This tenderizes and adds flavor. When done take fat meat out and skim grease off top. Make dough out of sweetmilk and roll it out like pie (real thin). Cut in strips, pinch strips off about 2 inches and drop in squirrel broth.

Mrs. Gertrude Smith

Frog Legs

If somebody has been frog gigging and brings you a mess, you can have a good supper or breakfast. The meat is white and tender. Wash it good and salt, pepper, and flour it. Fry like chicken. The legs will pop and bend like the frog was still living and spatter grease.

Mrs. M. H. Solomon

Boiled Eel

Four small eels, sufficient water to cover them; a small bunch of parsley. Choose small eels for boiling; put them in a pan with the parsley, and just sufficient water to cover them; simmer till tender. Take them out, pour a little parsley and butter over them, and serve in a tureen.

Mrs. Jeff Pickson

Terrapin

To prepare terrapin for cooking, plunge into boiling water and boil five minutes. Lift out of water with skimmer and remove skin from feet and tail by rubbing with a towel. Draw out head, and rub off skin. To cook terrapin—put in a kettle, cover with boiling salted water, add two slices each of carrot and onion, and a stalk of celery. Cook until meat is tender, which may be determined by pressing feet-meat between thumb and finger. The time required will be from thirty-five to forty minutes. Remove from water, cool, draw out nails from feet, cut under shell close to upper shell and remove. Empty upper shell and carefully remove and discard gall-bladder, sandbags, and thick, heavy part of intestines. Any of the gall-bladder would give a bitter flavor to the dish. The liver, small intestines, and eggs are used with the meat.

Mrs. Cecil Colquitt

How to Cook Possum

Parboil. Then put it in something to bake it. Peel some sweet potatoes. Put the potatoes in with the possum. Baste the potatoes and the possum with the possum juice. Cook until 'tater and possum are done.

Rose Reynolds

Possum and Sweet Taters

After you skin and clean the possum, trim all fat off the carcass. When you are ready to cook the possum, place it in a pan. Put an onion and an apple inside the possum. Then sprinkle with salt, pepper, and sage. Put enough water in the pan to keep the possum from scorching. Cover. Place in oven at low heat and steam for one hour. Uncover, place sweet potatoes around possum; replace cover and cook until potatoes are tender. Uncover and brown the possum.

Mrs. Cecil Colquitt

Braised Owl

Truss an owl as for roasting. Stuff the crop with good force-meat or sausage meat. Lay slices of bacon over the breast, and put in a braising pan as much good stock as will reach half way up the legs, two onions, and a small bundle of sweet herbs. Let it stew very gently until perfectly tender, then take it up, remove the bacon from the breast, and keep warm while you take the fat off the gravy, and reduce it by boiling without the lid of the pan to about one-half. Brush over the breast of the owl with glaze. Pour the gravy round and serve.

Mrs. Jeff Pickson

Pigeon Pie

Clean and cut each bird in four quarters. Line a deep dish with a good crust. Place a layer of thin slices of pickled pork at the bottom. On these put a layer of the birds—seasoned with pepper and salt sprinkled over them, butter the size of a walnut and cut in little pieces, and dust thickly with flour. Place another layer of birds and season as before.

When all the pigeon are in, cover the top with thin slices of pork, pour over all this a pint of broth, or if you have none, the same is to use water and cover with crust. Bake an hour in a moderate oven; leave an opening out each way in the middle of the top crust, if the pie seems dry add more broth. When the pie is done, cover it with an ornament of crust which you have baked separately on a pie dish or tin.

Mrs. Weida Daughtery

Brains and Eggs

One set calf or hog brains
Salt to taste
6 eggs

Scramble in butter or bacon fat.

Roberta Jackson

Scrambled Eggs and Brains

To prepare brains—wash, remove arteries and membranes. Soak 1 hour in cold water. Cook until water drains out then add eggs and scramble.

Mrs. Gertrude Smith

Deer Steak

Rip out underside of backbone of deer, stick on a forked stick and put on top of flame. Turn it till it gets almost done, take out and season, then place back in flame and turn till it gets real light brown and starts to drip. Gnaw it off the stick.

Josie Cora Thompson

Vegetables, Soups, Jellies, and Condiments

Vegetables grow abundantly in Alabama, and they have always provided the bulk of the main meal: turnips, collards, cabbage, wild poke salad, mustard, rutabagas, beets, peas, butterbeans, string or green beans, corn, okra, and tomatoes. Boiled for one to two hours, with bacon drippings and fatback for seasoning, they are reheated the next day or eaten cold for supper, canned or dried against the winter. Some folks claim biscuits taste better with collards but most Alabamians prefer our legendary cornbread with vegetables. The preparation of vegetables is tedious and lengthy—another reminder of the time, patience, and care involved in folk cookery where nothing is instant and nearly everything is good.

We learned that we had to *ask* people how to cook vegetables. Folks do not associate recipes, that is, specific measurements, ingredients, and instructions, with vegetables. You just cook them the way your mother and your grandmother—and *her* mother and grandmother—cooked them. Ask any lady in Alabama over sixty how to cook peas or turnips and we grant that she will be dumbfounded and amused at your ignorance.

Soups bear the signature of their folk makers. The cook "makes do" with what she has on hand, and she may omit or add ingredients according to her family's preference. (Peppers, onions, white potatoes, corn, peas, okra, and butterbeans are widely used in stews, soups, and gumbos, the stock varying: beef, chicken, fish, bacon fat, ham, goat, and fatback.) Yet, some broad traditions have evolved in Alabama. The recipes we collected are more properly gumbos or stews, thick concoctions of meat and vegetables, hearty and strengthening: calf's head and oxtail soup, boiled and boned meat of less desirable portions, chicken and dumplings, rich oyster soup and shrimp stew (fish appears in gumbo recipes, rather than independently, in this collection), White House Bouillon, oyster gumbo (made with cabbage and tomatoes instead of the usual top milk and cream), chicken stew prepared with ham, oysters, and spices, including sassafras, and famed Brunswick or Camp Stew, of controversial origin, made with hogshead and other parts at hog-killing time, rabbit, chicken, and goat.

Corn-meal gruel, a very thin soup made with either milk or water, is the classic food for infants, the sick, and convalescents. White sauce, made with milk, butter, and flour, poured over boiled white potatoes is another favorite for the sick, though the housewife prepared it just as often for the entire family, since it was filling and satisfying. Gravies are usually preferred to sauces: red-eye or ham gravy, thickening gravy, sawmill, milk, and chicken gravy.

Jams, jellies, preserves, and pickles round out the meal. Cucumbers, green and ripe tomatoes, peaches, pears, and cabbage are pickled and made into relishes. Domestic and wild fruits—plum, apple, persimmon, pear, peach, berries, watermelon, fig, scuppernong, muscadine—are the principal sources of jams, jellies, and preserves, though rosepetal jam and jelly were once quite popular. Preserving, pickling, and jelly making are, in reality, folk crafts; the recipe itself is only a verbal distillation of the process.

The tossed green salad that most Americans seem to prefer nowadays was not unknown to our grandparents; greens and onions in season were served with hot bacon drippings. But they did not have the various congealed salads that became popular with the advent of refrigeration. Salads as salads were not found on tables; instead, there was a plateful of onions, peppers, tomatoes, and radishes. In wintertime, cucumber and tomato pickles, vegetable and fruit relishes, and pickled pears and peaches took the place of salads.

Fried Beans

Wash and pick over one pound of pinto beans. (Let soak if you prefer.) Boil until tender, adding nothing until done. Then add salt. Mash beans (the amount you prefer to fry) then pour into hot bacon grease, and let fry until thoroughly mixed.

Dorothy Garcia

Old-Fashioned Baked Beans

Wash 4 cups of white beans and put to soak in water several hours, or over night. Put in pot and boil with several slices of salt pork until beans are tender, but not too soft. Then add salt to taste, a half cup of brown sugar and a half cup of molasses. Put in a good oven and bake until a rich brown.

Fried Blackberries

About a pint of blackberries
Some cold corn bread
Cooking oil—enough to cover the frying pan well.
Sugar

Wash berries, sweeten to taste. Cook until tender. Crumble enough cold corn bread to thicken juice. Have cooking oil (or bacon drippings) hot, then pour in above mixture, stirring until season is thoroughly cooked in.

Mrs. Fred Johnson

Fried Apples and Onions

Fry the onions in the usual way, but before they are thoroughly done, slice good tart apples into the pan and fry both together until the apples are done through. A dash of salt and a sprinkle of sugar adds to the flavor.

Betsy Allen

Baked Ash Potatoes

After an oak wood fire has been burned down and you have a lot of hot ashes put sweet potatoes in the ashes. Cover the potatoes with ashes. Keep hot potatoes cooked on top of the ashes. These potatoes are real good.

Mrs. Joe Hilson

Fried Cucumbers

Peel the cucumbers and slice the long way. Dry the slices, salt, pepper and flour. Fry in shortening until brown.

Elizabeth Berry

Fried Cucumbers

Pare the cucumbers, slice them about half an inch in thickness, lay them in ice water for fifteen or twenty minutes, then drain them and wipe each piece separately; season them with pepper and salt and dust them with flour; fry them in butter and lard, equal quantities of each. They should be sliced lengthwise.

Mrs. Weida Daughtery

Irish Potato Fritters

Peel and slice six medium   1 pinch salt
   sized Irish potatoes.   3 fingers of baking powder
1 handful plain flour

Mix the three ingredients until it makes a paste. Dip sliced potatoes into paste and drop into boiling grease—turn once. Place on brown paper.

Mrs. Frank Stephens

Scrambled Eggs and Onion

Chip spring onions (tops and roots) into a pan with seasoning and water. Cook until onions are tender and water is cooked out. Beat eggs and add to onions and scramble.

Mrs. Nichols

Fried Onion Rings

4 large onions   ½ cup flour
⅔ cup milk   Shortening for frying

Cut cleaned onions into ¼-inch slices and separate into rings. Soak onion rings in milk 10 to 15 minutes. Dredge rings in flour, then fry in deep fat heated on 365 degrees F. a few at a time, until well browned, about 2 to 3 minutes. Drain on paper toweling. Season and immediately serve.

Mrs. Florine Metcalf

Baked Redbeets

Scrub fresh beets thoroughly. Place in oven and bake till tender. Be careful not to prick them too much with fork as this allows the flavorful juices to escape. When done, peel and serve hot with bit of butter on top.

Annie Cooper

Poke Salad

Wash poke leaves real good. Boil up, pour off first water, then cook like turnips. Or you can use a few poke leaves in a mess of turnips and some green onions shoots. Cook down with a good bit of bacon drippings.

Louise Jolly

Hominy

Pour 1 qt. of water over ½ gal. oak ashes. Let drip until it drips about 3 cups. Put the drippings over 6 qts. of shelled corn. Pour over this 2½ gals. of water. Boil corn until tender. Wash several times.

Mrs. A. D. Watkins
Mary Olive Byrd

Tie some oak ashes in a rag and drop in a pot of shelled corn. Boil until the husk on the corn is loose. Pour off lye water and remove husks and kernels from corn. Add more water and boil until tender.

Alice Campbell

Hominy

Get corn, put in pot. Add about a teaspoon of lye to a gallon corn. Put in water to cover corn. Then boil corn tender and wash it until the eyes of the corn comes out. Boil again until tender. Take it up.

Lizzie Shields

Lye Hominy

½ gallon of ashes Oak or Hickory
1 gallon of corn
1 cup of salt

Put corn in container filled with water. Put ashes in light-weight bag.
Cook the corn until it husks, wash until the water is clear.

Mrs. Maddox
Sara Emfinger

Lye Hominy

Use oak, wood ashes from the fireplace, put in a barrel, pour water over
the ashes and make a hole in the bottom for the lye to drain out, cook
the lye and corn together.

Mrs. Margaret Crittenden

Hominy

Use one-half gallon oak ashes over which a quart of water is poured.
This is to stand over night (will be about three and a half cups to drip
out). This lye water is poured over six quarts of shelled good corn. Then
add about two and a half gallons of water. Let this boil real good for
about three hours or until the corn is tender. The corn is then washed
several times to remove some of the lye water. The corn can be seasoned with bacon drippings and fried for a few minutes, and is ready to
be served.

Mrs. J. W. Hodges

Hominy

Corn soaked over night in soda water, cook in some water until tender,
wash thoroughly until water is clear.

Mrs. T. L. Helms

Hominy Crescents

½ cupful hominy   ½ teaspoon salt
1 cupful boiling water   Dash of pepper
1 cupful milk   2 slightly beaten yolks

Add the hominy slowly to the boiling water, then salt and milk, and cook this in double boiler for 30 minutes, add yolks and pepper and mix thoroughly. Pour this into flat dish, rinsed with cold water, and leave until it is cold, then turn out and cut into crescent form with a cookie cutter. Dip each crescent in flour then into slightly beaten egg to which 1 tablespoon cold water was added, and then in sifted bread crumbs. Fry in deep fat until brown.

Mrs. J. H. Hankins

Okra*

Pick young tender pods if you can, especially for boiling. Wash, trim some of stem. Lay on top of peas or butter beans when they're about half done. Or, cook a pot separate. Add salt and bacon grease. Some folks like a good bit of black pepper with their boiled okra. To fry: same as you would green tomatoes and squash. Slice in circles, salt and pepper. Put some meal and maybe a little flour in a paper sack or clean, old flour sack. Shake good. Can either deep fat fry, or, if short of grease, sort of scramble in what you've got—cover the bottoms of the skillet at least.

Corn

Young tender white corn is best for boiling—just the nubbins or a little better. Cook more than you need—it won't go far. Use a big pot—boil just until tender—no need to add sugar, though some folks do. Put a little salt and some bacon grease in water—or wait until served and spread with a bit of butter. Suck cob for sweet juice. Medium firm yellow corn is best for roasting in shuck at low heat. To cream: pick at least a bushel for a family of six or to have a little left over for supper. Shuck in the yard—corn draws flies just like collards and cabbage. Get off as much silk as you can. Wash. Hold cob in left hand, pointed

---

Editor's Note: The recipes for okra, corn, rutabagas, peas, butterbeans, potatoes, turnips, mustard, dry peas and butter beans, cabbage, collards, beans, vegetable soup, cornbread and milk, are all from Mrs. M. H. Solomon.

earthwards. With sharp butcher knife slice off top of kernels from top to bottom. Repeat all the way around cob. Then, take knife and scrape, juice will splatter everywhere, so be sure and use a big mouth bowl or dish pan. Do this until you've scraped the bushel. *Set on low heat,* do not cook on high, it will stick if you don't stir it ever so often. May have to add a bit of water or milk, if it goes dry, not much. Add salt, sugar, especially if it's yellow corn, white corn creams the best, add a bit of bacon fat or butter. Keep cooking a long time on low heat. Serve with beans, butterbeans, okra, corn bread, *etc.* Best to cook in iron skillet—it won't stick so bad.

Rutabagas

Peel, wash, however many you need, they cook down. Slice in quarters or smaller, if you have time. Cook like turnip roots. Either lay meat on top or boil it awhile in little water before you add rutabagas. When tender, mash with fork. Serve with hot pepper sauce.

Peas

Different peas take different cooking times. A black-eye will cook out mushy, if you don't watch. Ladyfingers are little but hard. Field peas are about medium in color and everything else, a crowder makes out the most, a sugar crowder's got the best taste, young crowders make a light brown liquor, old, big crowders make it darker. Purple hulls stain the fingers and make a medium-brown liquor. Watch that purple hulls and old crowders don't go to mush. Shell a good mess, depending on how many will eat, whether you want some for supper or next day. Wash. Pick out the wormy ones, wash, be careful to get stuff from hulls off—this may take awhile. Cover with water (or boil up your meat first), lay white meat on peas, add however much bacon grease, sugar, and salt you want. Cook until tender. You may have to add water to get the liquor right. Serve with onion, pepper sauce, fresh hot pepper pods, one or all.

Butterbeans

Same as for peas, except butterbeans don't turn out as good as peas. Better if they're young and tender. White or green butterbeans take more time to cook. Old colored or speckled butterbeans will turn to mush if you cook too long.

New Potatoes

Scrape potatoes in a pan of cold water. Put on to boil in a little water, with a pinch of soda. Pour off first water, rinse, and start again to cook. Make you up a paste of plain flour and warm water in a teacup. Stir in flour paste real slow. Add sweet milk slow. Then, put in some butter. Sprinkle with black pepper. Good with green beans.

Sweet Potatoes

You can bake them on low heat, grease skin a little before putting in oven. Take what's left and make up custard or souffle or sweet potato biscuit. Or you can fry slices about ½ in. thick in bacon grease. Serve at breakfast with sausage or tenderloin.

Turnips

Trim roots from greens, set aside. Wash greens thoroughly in several waters, strip leaves from larger stems. Peel roots, wash, dice, halve, or leave whole. Set on a pot ⅓ full of water, bring to boil, add salt, add greens in two or three batches. As each batch cooks down, add another. When all greens are cooked down, add roots. (Wait awhile if roots are diced, since they take less time to cook that way.) Lay a good sized chunk of white meat (streak-of-lean) on top. (May use slices or a chunk that has been cut several times to the rind.) Sprinkle a little sugar over greens, especially if bitter. Add several spoons of bacon fat—greens need both meat and grease. Cook on low heat until greens are tender and deep dark color. If you want, greens and roots may be cooked separately. To serve: Pour up in bowl or large platter, cut up, crumble some cornbread and mix with greens, or, just before greens are done, drop in small portions of moist cornbread mixture. Or serve up plain, saving pot liquor to eat with crumbled-up cornbread next day or later that night. Skim off grease, smooth over greens, lay fat on top. You can boil up your white meat first for about half an hour, then put the greens in.

Mustard

Same as for turnips. Mix turnips and mustard, cook together if you haven't got enough of either one, or if you like them that way.

Dry Peas and Butterbeans

Soak dry peas or butterbeans overnight in cold water. Next morning pour off water, pick out wormy peas. Wash again. Set on to cook. Add salt, bacon dripping and several slices fatback. Cook just until tender. Won't take as long as fresh ones. Good with baked sweet potatoes.

Cabbage

Cabbage cooks down, it may take several heads for a large family—one to two medium cabbage for family of five. Remove outer leaves, wash, cut into four sections. Chip up, not as fine as for slaw. Put ½ to 1 cup water in pot, size depends on how many cabbage, can use small pot and add cabbage as they cook down. Bring water to boil, add a pinch of sugar and salt to taste. Add cabbage. Add however much bacon fat you want, not as much as for collards and turnips. Can just cook a few minutes until wilted or cook down for an hour.

Collards

Same as for turnips, except collards are tougher, need more grease and meat, and longer time to cook. Cook down more than turnips. Don't leave much liquor. Serve with cornbread, sweet potatoes, hot pepper sauce, and buttermilk.

Beans

Beans turn out real good. Some people like flat beans with the pea inside, others like round, juicy bright green beans, running or bush beans. Snap. Watch out for strings. Wash. Not so much washing as for greens, beans are usually clean. Boil just as for other vegetables. Some like a good bit of liquor, others like beans cooked down, takes a good bit of grease. You can add new potatoes—lay on top when beans are three-quarters done. Best to boil up new potatoes with a pinch of soda, pour off first water, rinse, and then set to cook—that way they won't make you sick. Spring beans are good with fresh onion, radish, lettuce, and cucumber. You can serve a vinegar relish with all vegetables. Put onion, pepper, and cucumber in a bowl, cover with vinegar, let stand a good long while, add pepper and salt if you want.

Vegetable Soup

Pick good ripe tomatoes. Peel or dip in hot water and skin, mash up good. Add some water. Put in what's left on the stove of the peas, butterbeans, okra and corn. Boil up, turn down quick or set off. Must cook slow or it'll stick. Add bacon fat, salt, sugar, pepper. You can start off fresh with all the vegetables, but it takes up a heap of time. Some folks call it gumbo. You can put it up in jars. It tastes good in the winter time.

Cornbread and Milk

Good for supper. Crumble up cornbread left from dinner in a bowl of sweet or buttermilk, whichever you like the best. Or, if there's no bread left, cook a fresh pan or fry some cakes on top of the stove. It's best to cook up enough to start with unless it's winter. Slice you some sweet white onion and eat with it, or chip up the onion in the bread and milk. If it's cold, follow it with a cup of coffee or sit by the fireplace to keep the chill off. Good with a slice of Georgia chicken too.

Bean Salad

Choose young snap beans for this salad. Either break into ½ in. pieces or leave whole. Cook until tender. When cool add onion rings, salt, pepper, and vinegar. Let this stay in the refrigerator over night. Before serving add some olive oil.

Mrs. Ruth Parks

Irish Potato Salad

Cook potatoes until done. Drain off the water and mash. Mix in several boiled eggs cut into small pieces and pickles chopped fine. Add salt and black pepper to taste.

Mrs. S. J. King

Wilted Green Salad

Wash and tear 2 quarts of fresh greens (lettuce, mustard, *etc.*). Mix with spring onions and radishes. Fry 4 slices of bacon until crisp, then

remove from pan. Put greens in the hot fat, and cook until wilted.
Season with a little vinegar; break bacon in bits and mix with the
leaves. Serves 4. Serve with hot corn bread and buttermilk.

Mrs. Earl Davis

Gumbo

Take an old chicken and cut up, breaking the bones when necessary.
The head and the feet are not to be used. Fry the chicken in deep fat
until it is light brown. Put the fried chicken in twice as much water as
you want soup, add 5 large slices of unboiled ham, a small onion cut
into slices, sweet herbs tied in a muslin bag, one small sliced carrot, 4
cloves, ½ teaspoon of all-spice, 3 pinches of salt, 1 pinch of nutmeg, ⅔
teaspoon of mace, and hot and white pepper. 1 tablespoon of young
sassafras, barely mature, but dried and pulverized. Simmer for a few
hours. When the chicken falls off the bones, take out the bag of herbs. A
few minutes before serving add a dozen large oysters and heat long
enough to plump them. Do not let sassafras boil. Serve over rice in a
soup bowl.

Mrs. Tom Coleman

Gumbo

Fry two fowls (old ones are best) with parsley, onions, pepper, salt and
lard or bacon. Put these into the pot with water sufficient for the soup,
and boil until the flesh drops off the bone. Just before taking off the fire
add your oysters, and, a few minutes after, a tablespoon of gumbo
powder or file; scraps of ham or sausage are an improvement. The
gumbo does not require boiling after the file is put in.

Mrs. Tom Coleman

Gumbo Chow

Boil the cabbage; take out and chop, very fine; sprinkle with a little
flour, and put into hot lard, with water enough to keep from burning.
Add one pint of oysters and oyster liquor, one teacup of tomatoes, and
salt and pepper to taste. Just before serving, add three tablespoonfuls
of molasses. Serve with rice boiled dry.

Mrs. Tom Coleman

Oyster Stew

½ pint of oysters in juice from oysters
Bring to boil
Add pint milk
Spoonful of chipped onions
Add 1 teaspoonful butter
Add 6 soda crackers, broken up

Carola Windham

Oyster Soup

To two quarts of strained oyster liquor, boiling, add one hundred
oyster, with salt and pepper to taste. Let all boil together till the edges
of the oysters curl, skimming constantly. Remove the oysters to the
tureen, and thicken the soup with one tablespoonful of flour rubbed in
two tablespoonfuls of melted butter. Boil in a separate vessel (to
prevent curling) one quart of sweet milk and pour in the tureen,
pouring in the soup last. Can be thickened with three hard-boiled eggs
rubbed smooth.

Mrs. Tom Coleman

Shrimp Stew

1 pt. milk, boiling hot
1 cup cream
Juice and grated rind of 1 lemon
Sherry wine
2 egg yolks, beaten

1 tablespoon flour mixed to a paste
  with a little milk
1 pt. shrimp, cooked and broken
  (not cut) into pieces

To the hot milk, pour in the cream. Lemon juice and rind, egg yolks,
flour paste, and shrimp. Flavor with wine and serve hot.

Catfish Stew

Cook the catfish till you can bone it then add Irish potatoes, green corn,
and some fresh tomatoes.

Mary Glenn Merritt

Brunswick Stew
(MADE AT HOG-KILLING TIME)

1 hog's head	Salt and pepper
1 hen or rabbit	1 pint of corn
1 quart of tomatoes	¼ pound of butter
1 big onion	Flour
1 pint of lima beans	4 or 5 potatoes
1 tablespoon sugar	

Cook the meat and take out the bones. Cut the meat in pieces. Put meat back in kettle with other things. Add salt and pepper to taste.

Mrs. Mary Price

Ox Tail Soup 1

Two ox tails, 2 slices of ham, 1 oz. of butter, 2 carrots, 2 turnips, 3 onions, 1 leek, 1 head of celery, bunch of savory herbs, 1 bay leaf, 12 whole peppercorns, 4 cloves, 1 tablespoon of salt, 2 tablespoonfuls of catsup, ½ glass of port wine, 3 quarts of water.

Cut and wash the tails, separating them at the joints, wash. Cut the vegetables in slices, add butter and tails all in a sauce pan with peppercorns and herbs. Put in ½ pint of water, and stir it over a sharp fire till the juices are done. Fill up the stew pan with the water, and, when boiling, add the salt. Skim well, and simmer very gently for 4 hours, or until the tails are tender. Take them out, skim and strain the soup, thicken with flour, and flavor with the catsup and port wine. Put back the tails, simmer for 5 minutes and serve.

Mrs. Jeff Pickson

Ox Tail Soup 2

The day before the soup is wanted take three ox tails, cut them in pieces and put them on to fry in butter, first removing all fat, let brown and set aside until the next day. Take off all grease from tails and boil in 3 quarts of water, add salt and pepper, onions, carrots, turnips and celery. Boil 4 or 5 hours.

Todd Pierce

Calf's Head Soup

Prepare a calf's head and take out the brains. Place the head in a kettle. Add one gallon of water. Boil it until it comes to pieces, then take out all the bones. Return the remains to vessel, adding on top of butter, one teacup of browned flour, 1 teacup tomato catsup, 1 tablespoon allspice and nutmeg, season with salt and pepper. When soup is ready, fry the brains and add. Before serving add 1 teacup of wine, 1 teaspoon of cloves along with some mace, sliced lemons and hard-boiled eggs.

Todd Pierce

Calf's Head Soup

After thoroughly cleaning the head, put it in a soup-kettle with a knuckle of veal which has been cut into several pieces, season with pepper and salt, four whole cloves, and a blade of mace; pour over all four quarts of cold water, bring to a boil, skim well and set aside to simmer, closely covered, for four or five hours; boil 2 eggs for 15 minutes, lay them in cold water for 5 minutes, then chop them and put in the tub in which you will serve the soup, with four or five slices of lemon, strain the soup, add a tablespoonful of browning and 2 glasses of Madeira or Sherry wine and serve.

Mrs. Weida Daughtery

White House Bouillon

Four pounds juicy beef, one knuckle of veal, two small turnips, two carrots, one soup bone, one small pod red pepper, two white onions, salt, six quarts of water. Boil six hours then strain through a sieve. Let stand overnight and congeal. Skim off the grease, put in a kettle to heat, and add sherry to taste.

Mrs. Tom Coleman

Chicken Stew

Cook chicken until tender, keep chicken covered in water. Add 3 tablespoons of good fresh butter and add 2 teaspoons of salt. Sift a mixing bowl half full of plain flour make a round in flour and add 1 cup sweet milk, salt, 2 tablespoons of grease and baking powder. Start mixing together with your hands, mix till hard enough to roll out ¼ of the dough at a time on floured rolling board or towel until thin and cut into small strips and drop in chicken and cook until tender, about 10 minutes. Cool and serve.

Mrs. Florine Metcalf

Soup Croutons

Cut slices of buttered bread into cubes and crisp in a hot oven. Drop in the soup just before serving or serve with it.

Mrs. Tom Coleman

Tomato Bisque

Cook one pint of tomatoes until thoroughly done, strain and add a pinch of salt; set aside on the stove, keeping it hot. Take a quart of sweet milk; let it come to the boiling point, then thicken with one tablespoonful of flour, creamed with a heaping tablespoonful of butter. Keep tomatoes and milk in separate vessels until ready to serve, then stir in one half teaspoonful of soda in the tomato juice and pour it slowly into the milk, stirring constantly.

Mrs. Tom Coleman

Cream-of-Celery Soup

Two bunches of celery cut fine and boiled until tender; strain through a colander. Mix with it one pint of stock, one cup of milk, and one cup of rich cream; season with salt and pepper. If not thick enough, add just a little flour dissolved in milk.

Mrs. Tom Coleman

Split-Pea Soup

Take three pints split peas, some stale bread and one turnip, sliced. Wash the peas and steep them in fresh water at least twelve hours; place them over the fire; add the bread, turnip, and a pinch of sugar; boil till all are quite soft; rub them through a fine colander adding gradually boiling water; return the soup into pan and boil a few minutes.

Mrs. I. L. Dann

Gruel Soup

About a qt. water
Small chunk butter

Meal to thicken
Salt and black pepper to taste

Mrs. T. L. Helms

Meal Soup

1 cup of milk
½ cup of meal
Dash salt and pepper

Cook until slightly thickened.

Mrs. Virginia Eiland

Corn Soup

Take fresh green corn about a half dozen ears . . . cut off the kernels and
boil the cobs in two quarts of water. When boiled, add the kernels and
cook until done. Season well with salt, pepper and the spices you like.
Keep boiling; add a cup of milk, stir in a tablespoonful of flour rubbed
in butter to thicken.

Garnishes for Clear Soup

For Julienne soup: To each quart of clear soup add one third cup each
of carrots and turnips cut into strips an inch long and about the
thickness of a match and boiled in water till tender.

For Macaroni Soup: To each quart of clear soup add half a cup of
macaroni cooked in boiling salted water till tender, and cut into rings.

Mrs. Tom Coleman

Fruit Relish

2 cups cranberries
2 cups brown sugar
2 oranges
2 cups raisins

½ cup cider vinegar
½ tsp. cloves
Three quarters teaspoon cinnamon
½ teaspoon salt

Put cranberries through food chopper or cut in halves. Add orange pulp and rind, sugar, salt, raisins, and vinegar. Cook fifteen minutes or until thick. Add spice and cook five minutes. Pour in glasses to cool.

Miss Willie Dismukes

Tomato Catsup

4 qts. strained tomatoes
6 tablespoon salt
3 tablespoons black pepper
1 tablespoon ground cloves

2 tablespoon ground cinnamon
2 tablespoon ground all-spice
1½ pints vinegar

Place in kettle and boil down to half of original quantity. Pour in sterilized [jars].

Miss Willie Dismukes

Milk Gravy

Brown a cup of meal in bacon grease. Add a dash of salt and pepper. Stir the meal until it is light brown. Pour sweet milk into the browned meal. Stir. Let the milk simmer until it is the desired thickness. Serve over hot grits on a cold night.

Mrs. Pauline Allen

Brinel Gravy

You mix some grease (cooking grease that you used at breakfast), and a little bit of already-made hot coffee in a scillit, and then you take it out of the pot or scillit and put it on biscuits.

Mrs. Louise Thomas

Red-Eye Gravy

Pour water or, better, strong black coffee, into the skillet where you cooked the ham. Let it boil up. Serve over grits and biscuits.

Mrs. Mackie Pienezza

Saw-Mill Gravy and Georgia Chicken

Soak fatback in cold water a few hours. Pour off. Dredge slices in flour. Fry, as chicken, turning often. Pour off most of grease. Stir in some flour, brown, then add water, let boil up, add black pepper.

Mrs. Ida Hornsby

Chicken or Thickening Gravy

Pour off most grease. Brown a little flour in bottom of skillet, add salt and pepper. Pour in milk, or water, or a mixture of these. Stir and pour off. Serve over biscuits or rice. Can heat left-over fried chicken in this gravy.

Mrs. Ida Hornsby

Old-Fashioned Plum Sauce

One gallon plums
4 pounds sugar

One cup vinegar
Two tsp. all-spice

Cover plums with water. Boil ten minutes, drain, add vinegar and sugar, cook thirty minutes before removing from fire, drop in spices tied in a bag. Remove spice bag and bottle. This is delicious with meat.

Grandmother's Sauce

Cream together a cupful of sifted sugar and a half of a cup of butter, add a teaspoon of ground cinnamon and an egg, well beaten. Boil a tea cup full of milk and slowly turn it, boiling hot over the mixture, stirring all the time, (this will cook the egg). The sauce will be smooth and may be served warm or cold.

Elizabeth Berry

Blackberry Jelly

Pick ripe blackberries and enough red ones to add acid, wash well and mash up, boil without water slow until berries come to pieces. Strain through flour sack and squeeze out all juice into dish pan. Add 1 cup sugar to 1 cup juice. Cook and skim off foam until it jellies in a saucer. Pour into jars and seal, place on window sill or water shelf on back porch for three or four days to finish jelling.

Note: Some cooks use ⅔ cup sugar to 1 cup juice.

Mrs. M. H. Solomon

Blackberry Jam

Pick ripe blackberries, wash and mash. Add 1 cup sugar to 1 cup berries. Cook on low heat until it jellies in saucer. Pour in jars and seal.

Mrs. M. H. Solomon

Peach and Pear Preserves

Peel ripe peaches, can set in hot water and skin will come off real easy. Chip up into cooking vessel, will be juicy. Add ⅔ to 1 cup sugar to every cup fruit. Cook over medium heat till syrup thickens and fruit turns color. (If peaches are real sweet and ripe, can add lemon juice or some peaches not too ripe, for acid.) Stir and skim off foam. Pour into hot jars and seal. Don't fool with jars until next morning. Listen for the pop. Make pear preserves the same way. Pears are tougher and make a good bit less juice. They'll turn about the color of rutabagas when ready. Add lemon juice and rind for acid.

Mrs. Harriette Norrell

Apple Jelly

Wash apples, cut into sections, put in vessel, core, skin, and all, simmer in a little water until tender. Strain juice through flour sack. Squeeze it good. Add ¾ to 1 cup sugar to 1 cup juice, some lemon juice, cook up, skim off foam, till it jells on saucer, pour in hot jars. Apple jelly is hard to make do. Tart apples take more sugar.

Mrs. Georgia Darden

Plum Jelly

Wash your plums, put in vessel with just enough water to keep from sticking. Can use wild plums or domestic or can mix. Boil up and simmer till fruit comes to pieces. Strain through flour sack. Add 1 cup sugar to 1 cup juice. Cook over medium fire, skim off foam, till it jellies. Pour in hot jars. Jelly will be red or orangish, depending on what kind of plums used.

Mrs. Loreli Ballard

Muscadine Jelly

Wash 'em. 1 gal. muscadines. Mash pulp out. Cover pulp with water. Cook until tender. Strain through cheese cloth, twice. Measure juice. Use one cup of juice to one cup of sugar. Cook until when tested in cool water it jellies. Pour into pint jars and seal. Cover hulls with water and cook until tender. Pour into quart jars and seal. Use to make pies.

Mrs. O. G. Causey

Wild Rose Jelly

Put 2 quarts wild rose petals in a kettle with 2½ quarts of cold water. Bring the water slowly to a boil and boil 15 minutes. Strain the liquor through a jelly bag and add to the extracted juice ½ cup strained fresh strawberry juice and enough water to make 2 quarts in all. Add 7 pounds sugar, stir until dissolved and bring to a rolling boil. Pour in quickly 2 cups liquid fruit pectin, stirring while pouring. Let the jelly boil briskly for 1 minute, pour hot into sterilized glasses and seal with paraffin. Store in a dark, cool, dry place.

Merton Reeves

Rose Petal Jam

To each cup of petals add 1 cup of water and 1 cup of sugar. Boil until sugar hardens on a wooden spoon. Add a few drops of lemon juice and a pinch of tartaric acid. If this is not done just at jellying time, the jam becomes bitter. Place jam in small glasses and cool before sealing with paraffin.

Merton Reeves

Rose Hip Jelly

For every pound of rose hips add one-half pint of water. Boil until the fruit is tender. Then pass through a fine sieve to keep back the seeds. Add one pound of pulp, and boil until it jellies. The rose hips should have been touched by the frost before being made into jelly.

Watermelon Preserves

10 lbs. melon rind
10 lbs. sugar
1 cup cinnamon bark
3 t. lime

½ cup salt
7 qts. water
¼ lbs. ginger root

Annie Blake

Old Fashioned Fig Preserves

Weigh figs and wash in clear water. Drain well. Layer figs with a generous layer of sugar. A pound of sugar to a pound of figs. Alternate until pan is nearly full. Cover and let set over night. Cook *slowly*, until figs are tender and the syrup is slightly thickened. Can remove figs from juice, boil up juice, drop figs in to cook. It's slower, but figs will not go to pieces that way. Some folks like them cooked long, the figs will be dark brown and nearly candied, others like them medium brown in a light syrup. Place in sterilized pint jars and seal.

Mrs. I. W. Brown,
given to Louise Jolly

Strawberry Preserves

Take a pound of nice ripe berries; add a pound of granulated sugar. Mix together in an enameled kettle or pan and put on stove. Cook slowly until they come to a boil about 20 minutes. Lift out berries with a skimmer and put in heated fruit jars. Leave a little space at top of jar. Then bring the juice left in the kettle to a boil for four or five minutes. Pour it hot over berries in jars. They should be sealed while hot and kept in a cool, dry place. My, but they're delicious that way!

To Preserve Barberries in Bunches

Barberries; to every pint of juice allow a pound and a half of loaf sugar, and to every pound of sugar half a pound of barberries in bunches. Select the finest barberries, taking the largest bunches to preserve whole. Pick the rest from the stalks, and put them into a preserving-pan, with sufficient water to make a syrup for the bunches; boil them till they are soft, then strain them through a hair sieve, and to every pint of juice put a pound and a half of pounded sugar. Boil and skim it well, and to every pint of syrup put a half a pound of barberries, tied in bunches. Boil them till they look very clear, then put them into pots or glasses, and when cold, tie them down with paper dipped in brandy.

Watermelon Honey

10 lbs. chopped melon rind
2 lemons

2 quarts cold water
¼ lb. preserved ginger or ginger root

Aimie Johnson

Recipe for Cabbage Kraut

To make brine, put salt in boiling water until it is strong enough to float an egg. Quarter cabbage heads and drop into a crock of cooled brine. Cover with a cloth to keep out insects. This is the way to pickle meat, too.

Mrs. J. J. Beard

Pokeberry Pickles

In the spring when the poke is tender and after you have gathered the leaves for "greens," you break the tenderest stalks into the desired lengths and scald in boiling water. Drain (poke can be poisonous). Skin the stalks and place in jars. Add hot vinegar, plain or add any spices you like for example, cloves, allspice, *etc.* Seal the jars you want to store for later.

Mrs. J. H. Duke

Green Tomato Pickle

Use 5 lbs. solid green tomatoes (size to go in pint jar easily).
1. Slice ¼ in. thick and soak in 2 gallons of lime water 24 hours. (3 cups lime to 2 gallons of cold water)
2. Wash carefully and drain. Soak in clear water 12 hours.
3. Drain and soak 24 hours in alum water. (1 box alum to 2 gallons water)
4. Rinse and soak 3 or 4 hours in ginger tea. (1 box ground ginger with enough water to make a paste. Add enough cold water to well cover the tomatoes, mixing ginger paste before adding tomatoes)

Syrup:

3 pints red vinegar	1 teaspoon ground allspice
5 lbs. sugar	1 teaspoon ground ginger
1 teaspoon ground cloves	1 teaspoon celery seed

Mix in enamel dish pan, add green tomatoes—let stand covered overnight. Bring to a boil *slowly* and cook *slowly* 1 hour. Put in jars and seal.

Louise Jolly, given to
her by Frances Nelson

Pear Relish

1 peck pears	5 large onions
5 green peppers	5 c. vinegar
5 red peppers	5 c. sugar
2 or 3 hot pepper pods	1 t. salt

Grind up pears in food chopper. Drip off excess juice. Then, put peppers and onions through grinder. Combine with vinegar, sugar, and salt, bring to boil, and boil 20 minutes. Seal in hot, sterilized jars.

Mrs. Harriette Norrell

Cucumber Pickle

8 lbs. cucumber, sliced in rounds	2 qts. vinegar
2 cups household lime	9 cups sugar
2 gal. water	2 tbsp. salt

Soak cucumbers overnight in lime and water, use crock or enameled pan. Remove from lime water, wash through 3 changes of fresh, cold water. Mix vinegar, sugar, and salt, put drained cucumber slices in mixture for three hours, then bring to a boil and boil for 30 minutes. Seal in hot, sterilized jars.

Mrs. Harriette Norrell

Pickling Meat

Cut meat up the same day the hog is butchered. Salt real good and spread out over night until well chilled. The next morning peek in barrel, placing a layer of salt. Make a strong brine and let stand until cold. The third day you pour the brine over the meat until covered. Let stand until the meat absorbs the brine well. Fill wash pot with water to boil. Add red pepper to water. Dip meat in boiling water. Hang and smoke with oak or bay wood. Smoke only a few pieces at a time.

Mrs. Sallie Seay

Sweet Pear Pickle

7 lbs. peeled pears	½ oz. cloves
3 lbs. sugar	½ oz. stick cinnamon
1 pt. apple vinegar	1 oz. all-spice

Mix sugar, vinegar, and spices. Bring to boil. Drop in pears. Cook until tender. Pack with sufficient syrup in hot, sterilized jars.

Willie Davis

Tomato Relish

A peck of ripe tomatoes
6 green peppers
6 large onions
1 ½ pts. vinegar
1 cup brown sugar

2 ½ tb. salt
1 tb. ginger
1 tb. mustard
2 tb. cinnamon

Mash up tomatoes, remove core. Chop onions and peppers. Put all in vinegar and spice mixture. Cook in large kettle or dish pan several hours on low heat, stirring often, until thickened. Pack in hot, sterilized jars.

Mrs. Harriette Norrell

Chow-Chow

1 gal. chopped cabbage
½ gal. chopped green tomatoes
a doz. or so onions

4—6 red sweet peppers
4—6 green sweet peppers

In crock or enamel dish pan put a layer of mixture, sprinkle with salt, then another layer and salt, let stand over night, drain, make up a vinegar solution, about a gallon, with 2 lbs. sugar and spices, mustard, cloves, and celery. Put cabbage mixture in after it comes to a boil, then cook slow for about a half hour. Pack in hot, sterilized jars.

Mrs. Harriette Norrell

Pepper Hash

12 red peppers
12 green peppers
12 small onions size (of) small egg

3 pints vinegar
2 tablespoonfuls salt
2 cups sugar

Chop peppers and onions fine, pour boiling water over them and let stand five minutes. Boil vinegar, sugar and salt then add peppers and boil up once—seal while hot.

Mrs. Ruth Herren

Recipes from the papers of Mrs. A. L. Harlan

Women tuck recipes here and there, sometimes between the pages of their favorite cookbook. In the Alabama Room of the Russell Library at Alexander City State College we discovered among the papers of Mrs. A. L. Harlan a number of old handwritten recipes in a 1906 cookbook (*Woman's Favorite Cook Book,* Chicago, International Publishing Co., edited by Annie R. Gregory). A number of the recipes were dated much earlier than the book. One entry reads: *"Recipies* collected by Papa while in New York, Summer 1882." The handwriting is that of Mrs. Harlan, who signs her name together with "Ashland, Ala. Aug. 8 1889."

Strawberries

Carefully pick over your fruit, then place in your glass jars. Add to each quart of fruit one cup of sugar. Now place in your boiler a board with a few holes bored through to allow the water to pass under the jars. Put on this board all the jars the boiler will hold, then put cold water in until it comes within two inches of the top of the jar. Place the boiler on the top of the stove, and after it reaches the boiling point, allow it to boil twenty minutes. Put your rubbers and tops in warm water, and as you take each jar from the water, seal at once, first filling *full* with a syrup of sugar and water—this of course must be hot. As your fruit gradually cools, tighten your tops. Do not put away until thoroughly cold—then put in a cool dry place & cover to exclude the light—thus preserving the original color of the fruit.

Canned Tomatoes

They must be entirely fresh and not over ripe. Pour boiling water over them, drain off and remove the skins. Slice into a porcelain kettle—cook for twenty minutes in their own juice—skim the scum which rises, have the cans hot and fill with hot tomatoes. Wipe can tops and rubbers *dry,* and *tighten gradually.* When cold, set in dark place.

Canned Peaches

To peel, drop into boiling water for a moment, then into cold water and strip off the skin. (This saves both fruit and labor). After pealing, stone and place in a steamer over a kettle of boiling water. Make a syrup of one cup of white sugar to each cup of fruit. Steam fruit until easily pierced with a broom splint. Fill the jar nearly full of fruit and turn syrup over all and seal.

These directions for a domestic craft, written nearly a hundred years ago, are specific, meticulous, orderly, the attitude scientific—striking qualities in Alabama folk recipes, which are usually ambiguous, disordered, and imprecise, though the process itself is quite the reverse. Apparently the Yankee know-how in this matter impressed the Alabama gentleman favorably, since he went to the trouble of careful notation and reporting. However, all the other recipes in Mrs. Harlan's hand (which we have transcribed as faithfully as possible) are evidently of Southern circulation: White Fruit Cake, Black Fruitcake, other Fruit Cake, Gold Spice Cake, East Cake Bread, Strawberry Acid, and Rummage Pickles. Mrs. Harlan may, of course, have kept other recipes, but it is interesting that this particular group consists mostly of foods associated with traditional Christmas celebrations.

Folk cooking, like other folk crafts, is handed down from one generation to the next by actual example and practice. Committing a recipe to writing, translating it into a verbal structure, nearly always indicates a special significance: it is complicated or lengthy or both; it is prepared rarely, for certain social festivities; or the writer wishes to keep it in permanent form, to swap out with her friends, to pass along to relatives, or to preserve for her children. And so she "sticks it in a safe place"—in the Bible, in a scrapbook, in her sewing box, in an autograph album, in the trunk—along with her other personal papers, letters, diaries, newspaper notices of births, marriages, deaths—for the written recipe was also a treasure, a symbol of the family life that she nurtured and guarded.

Not many years ago we stopped at a fine, unpainted, weatherbeaten farmhouse where there were scores of people going in and out. We were told that a lady in her nineties had died and the children were "selling her stuff." What we saw was memorable in heartbreak—there were her preserves and jams, her canned tomatoes and beans, her hand-embroidered linens trimmed in crocheted lace, her quilts, her dishes, crockery, cooking vessels, her kerosene lamp, all with a price tag. A distracted hound dog prowled miserably at the steps, her cat leaped frantically from the porch railing. We never knew her name, but we sorrowed for her. The mobility of the twentieth century has brought estate, rummage, and garage sales—the remnant is scattered, and we are the poorer for it. The folklorist and the historian do not ask for slavish admiration of the past, but rather for careful study and honest judgment; without mementos, we can have neither. We have included here Mrs. Harlan's handwritten recipes because they reveal yet another rewarding way of searching out the life of the folk in Alabama.

White Fruit Cake

1 cup butter	1 grated coca.
2 cups sugar	½ lb. Eng. Wal. shelled
3 cups flour	½ lb blanched almon
Whites 8 eggs	½ raisins
1 cup sweet milk	½ lb pecans

Bake four hours

Black Fruit Cake
Dec. 18   1906

½ lb. crushed sugar	¼ cup syrup
½ lb butter	¼ tumbler brandy
½ lb flour (or more)	1 lb currants
6 eggs—broken sep	¾ lb. citron
1 teaspoon each pow—	1 lb. raisins
cloves—cin—nut spice	

Cooks in about 2 hrs so Annie says.

Pearl's East Cake Bread
Sept–1910

1 East cake dissolved in 1 cup water about 4 oclock p.m. in a tea cup—at night take 37 cups water 6 sp sugar (Table sp.) & lard size of an egg and work to a stiff dough & set to rise overnight in preserving kettle. In the a.m. right after breakfast knead and beat well and make into loaves and set to rise and bake; about 11 oclock.

Fruit Cake   Mrs. Park's

Cream together 1 lb. Sugar
  ¾ lb. Butter
Add some eggs well beaten
2 Table Sp Molasses
Whip one level T. Sp and let (?) dissolve
1 Lb. flour
1 glass (wine) milk
1 lb Raisons
1 lb Currants
2 Oz. Citron
1 Nutmeg
1 T. Sp Cinnamon
1 T. Sp Cloves
½ lb figs
Chop up ½ glass of almonds and add to it.

Gold Spice Cake

Yolks 7 eggs	1 Teaspoon Soda
1 Whole egg	5 cups flour
2 cups brown Sugar	1 T. Sp cloves
1 cup Molasses	2 T. Sp Cinnamon
1 cup Butter	2 T. Sp Ginger
1 cup Soup Milk	1 nutmeg

Mix eggs and butter
Add molas flour & milk late
Add nuts if you care to

Plum Pudding

2 cups bread crumbs,
   browned and sifted
2 cups flour
1 full cup suet or butter
1 lb. raisins
¼ lb. citron
1 teaspoon salt
¾ cup sugar

2 eggs (4 if you like)
1 teaspoon cinnamon
1 teaspoon vanilla
1 teaspoon lemon
1 teaspoon rrst (?)
⅕ teaspoon cloves
1 round teaspoon soda, 2 cups milk

Steam four hours.
This is fine.

(Signed) Pearl Ingersoll

Strawberry Acid

Dissolve four ounces of tartaric acid in two quarts of water (cold) and pour it over two gallons of ripe strawberries: let stand twenty four hours, and drain the liquor off: to every pint of Juice add a pound and a half of loaf sugar, boil, let stand three days and bottle. A few spoonfuls in a glass of ice water makes a delightful drink.

In making blackberry acid I use a little more tartaric acid & not quite so much sugar as recipie calls for.

Fruit Cake

1 lb. sugar—1 lb. butter
1 lb. flour—12 eggs
1½ teasp. Bak. Powder (or 2)
1 lb. Dates
1 lb. Raisons
1 lb. Currants

1 lb. citron
2 sp. Cinnamon
1 sp. Allspice
1 sp. cloves
½ cup Brandy

Rummage Pickle

2 Ripe cucumbers
1 qt. Green tomatoes
2 qt. Ripe tomatoes
1 Bunch Celery
1 cabbage

Green sweet peppers and onions
2 lb. Sugar
1 qt. vinegar
mustard, spices
Fresh Cucumbers ½ gal

[Written in very small type on side of page is another recipe.]

Tomato Relish

2 gal. Tomatoes	3 qt. vinegar
2 bunches celery	½ gal. cucumbers
1 qt. onions	4 green (finger) peppers
2 medium cabbages	2 Tablesp mustard
1 qt. onions	1 teasp. cloves
3 lb. sugar	

Olivia Solomon's note to Rummage Pickle: Mrs. Harlan kept a little history of her pickling from 1911 to 1924. The entries, written on two small yellowed sheets, indicate that making Rummage Pickles was a sort of social ritual for the lady, her friends, and kinswomen. Nearly always they are made near her birthday, once "after returning from state W.M.U. convention in Montgomery," and on another occasion "the night after my return from U.D.C. at Savannah Nov. 24th (1924). Often she notes the weather; "Hard freeze Nov. 9—killed vegetation and flowers (Friday night of the Dis. Fed. of Clubs"— 1923; and again: "Had first killing frost on Monday night." On November 1 and 2 1911, she notes "Coz's Fannie and W. J. Street spend the day with us (my birthday, 1st Nov.)" but the 1912 entry reads: "Made Pickle Nov. 1st and finish Nov. 2nd again—Coz. Fannie sick in bed this time. Present U.D.C. crosses on Nov. 1st—Birthday." Some of our readers will remember a softer time when sisters, friends, and kinfolks came to "spend the day," a most pleasant custom that has almost disappeared. In the days when transportation was slow and difficult, and families lived several miles apart, a day-long visit was a longed-for, happy time that relieved the tedium, hard work, and loneliness of daily life. A great aunt of mine used to say to my grandmother Ida, "Sister, I've been so hungry to see you!" The need for companionship can, indeed, be a hunger, which our ancestors satisfied with church-going, revivals, quilting bees, and spend-the-days. While the children played, the ladies cooked dinner, talked to their heart's content, sewed, quilted, embroidered, and made pickles and preserves. Jack's father used to tell about going to spend the day with Aunt Matilda Roach—how his parents rose long before daybreak, loaded the children in the wagon bed and set off a distance of 10 or 12 miles. The kitchen was attached to the house, and Mr. Solomon praised his kinsmen as "good livers" who set a fine table, his Aunt the best cook in Crenshaw County. Mrs. Harlan's short diary is a touching reflection of those days. A ragged scrap of yellowed paper often holds the story of an entire culture.

Asfidity (Asafetida, Asafoetida)

ALABAMA FOLK REMEDIES

The folk remedies of Alabama, like the folk recipes, are dependent on readily available ingredients—the fruits, vegetables, plants, trees, herbs, and fauna native to our soil, and those products distributed through peddlers, country stores, mail order catalogs, and the ubiquitous "rolling store," a familiar part of our landscape until the '50s. Ingenious and, for the most part, sensible and curative, they are neither unique nor new—their use was widespread all over the United States in the nineteenth century and their origins date back to the beginning of recorded history, particularly to the ancient Egyptians and Greeks, who laid the broad foundations of medical theory and practice and of pharmacology. Some of the remedies, notably the use of gold and leeches, may be traced directly to medieval medical treatises and related secular literature. Those that are prescribed as blood purifiers reflect the medieval postulate of the "four humors" derived from the writings of the Greek physician Galen. In their insistence on talismans and amulets, chants, and magical transference, these remedies clearly identify their descent from European witchcraft and even from primitive rites wherein high priests exorcised the evils and diseases of the body.

In frontier Alabama every housewife was her own doctor. Real doctors, those trained to surgery and the known uses of current drugs, were to be found only in cities. Their imitators, the quacks and frauds who traveled from one small settlement to another, often brought harm to ignorant patients, and the peddlers of patent medicines were accomplished confidence men who gulled the folk into buying their purportedly miraculous tonics, cure-alls, liniments, salves, and lotions. Flamboyant in their style and oratory, they often came to town in a "phisik wagon," accompanied sometimes by dwarfs, freaks, and musical entertainers, sideshows for products such as this one:

De Bing's

Remedy

VIAFUGA

("The way to fly" for Relief)

The Pure Juices of Barks
Herbs, Roots and Berries

for

CONSUMPTION

Pneumonia, Pleurisy, Asthma, Bronchitis, Croup, Diptheria, Catarrh,
Whooping Cough, Gout
Sudden colds & Inflammation of the Lungs
For all those weaknesses and

AFFLICTIONS PECULIAR TO WOMEN

For Torpid and Deranged Conditions of the
Liver, Stomach, Bowels and Kidneys

producing

Dyspepsia, Costiveness, Diarrhoea, Dysentery, Cholic, Cholera, Morbus,
Spasms, Gravel, Dropsy, Scrofula, Syphilis
Congestive Chills, Ague and Fever

Copyrighted by L.F. Bingham
Washington, D.C., *1866*

DR. SPERRY'S CARD

Baltimore Mo. Jan. 1, *1868*

Having become familiar with the formula of DeBing's Via Fuga, I recommend it for consumption and its long train of attendant complaints,
knowing it to be the juices of Barks, Herbs, Roots and Berries.

M. M. Sperry, M.D.

Incipient Consumption Washington, D.C. Feb. 10, *1869*

I was long time troubled with a severe cough and peculiar female complaint, prostrating my system with night sweats. Your medicine has
strengthened me to a remarkable degree, and relieved me of cough,
chills, night sweats and nervous complaints. I am gaining flesh, and
thankful beyond my poor expression.

Mrs. Felicia Hill

Scro-fula Washington, D.C. Jan. 1, *1870*

I was afflicted with a terrible Scrofulous and syphilitic complaint, causing complaint, causing running sores and ulcers on my body. After
taking De Bing's wonderful remedy four weeks, I am completely cured of
that loathsome and disgraceful disease.

M. M. W.

Midwives, conjurers, and herb women were consulted in matters such as childbirth, skin eruptions, and more serious sicknesses that defied home treatment and peddler's miracle cures, but most ill-nesses—the plagues of infancy and childhood, mumps, measles, who-oping cough, colic, "hives," chicken pox, colds, corns and bunions, digestive ailments, puny systems, parasites, boils and carbuncles,

HERB WOMAN

rheumatism, burns, wounds, urinary disturbances, fevers and head-aches—responded, at least symptomatically, to a wide variety of common-sense prescriptions. That is, *most* of the remedies are common-sense ones. A few of them are not only bizarre but, if followed, might well prove fatal. One remedy for high blood pressure calls for pulling the hair up into a tight plait, sticking a match into it, and lighting it! The illnesses themselves range over the entire world of human physical frailty, and there are remedies for almost all of them. But some diseases have no folk cure: consumption, nearly always mortal and protracted, injuries which would obviously result in death, undefined wasting diseases (though there are a few for cancer, mostly skin cancer and one late remedy for internal cancer), and psychologi-cal disturbances, whether simple "bad nerves" or severe mental breakdowns and outright lunacy.

These exceptions are interesting: First, they imply a realistic attitude toward disease and the inevitability of death that we do not possess today. And nowhere is there evidence of the morbid attitude that characterized late Victorian necrology. That mournful spirit is reserved for funeral customs, songs, and tales. Second, in an environment where man struggled for sheer physical survival, the afflictions of the spirit and mind naturally received less attention than those of the body.

Though it might be rash to offer judgment, some scholars of psychology have observed that the number and intensity of mental aberrations are considerably lower in a frontier society dominated by a work ethic—except, of course, in cases of mass temporary hysteria such as the Great Awakening revivals in the nineteenth-century South and West and the witchcraft frenzy of Puritan New England. It is true that lunatics were held in fear and ridicule, that the stigmata of any unusual affliction marked its sufferer for exile. Yet literature also reveals instances in which the insane, the feeble-minded, and the emotionally disturbed were treated with kindliness and compassion. Perhaps a tentative conclusion can be drawn: our great grandparents squarely faced the truth that some diseases cannot be cured; hence, all remedies are useless. Yet, deep within and beyond these remedies, one can read the despair, and the hope, of an age in which the death of infants and mothers in childbirth, death from common childhood diseases, instant death from injuries, from malnutrition, malaria, and typhoid were all common occurrences, not rare ones as they are in our day when medicine has found true miracle cures.

Reading over these remedies and surveying the epitaphs on tombstones of any cemetery a century old is a deeply moving experience for the folklorist. The efforts of the human spirit to preserve its flesh and kindred in the face of overwhelming odds are blinding in their revelation of love—a mother nursing her fatally ill child with a poultice of turpentine and hog lard, with a cup of watermelon-seed tea, headstone after headstone with the names of infants who lived one day or a few months, of children who died in all the brightness of two and three years, of brothers who died the same day from diphtheria. The wisdom of the folk is expressed in their proverbs, their gaiety and joy in games, jokes, riddles and dances, their delight in story-telling, tall tales, ghost narratives, and legends, their passions in ballad songs, their cultural rites and practices in poetic superstitions; but their struggle to live is nowhere more poignantly suggested than in their remedies and gravestone carvings.

The dominant modes of treatment that emerge here are: teas and syrups, poultices, ointments, talismans, and magical transference. The available medicines that can be broadly classified as drugs include whiskey, quinine, laudanum, paregoric, belladonna, and morphine. Teas and syrups, administered for practically every illness, are compounded of roots, barks, and leaves (elms, red oaks, briar root and snake root, mullein and red clover leaves, pine needles, watermelon and peach seeds among the most popular); spices and herbs (orange peel, cloves, camomile, sassafras, columbine, fever-grass, catnip, mustard); sugar, water, and whiskey; and turpentine. Syrups, as purgatives, tonics, cough and sore-throat relievers, often use a base of honey or molasses, mixed with vinegar, turpentine, kerosene, and oil of castor. Poultices, applied directly to sprains and similar injuries, and most important in the treatment of croup, pneumonia, and other respiratory illnesses, consist of clay and animal fat (usually hog lard) combined with vinegar, turpentine, and kerosene. Turpentine, kerosene, and whiskey were staple medicines found in every home, taken internally and applied externally—the classic Alabama remedy for a child's cold is turpentine and lard rubbed on the chest and throat and for a nail in the foot (an almost daily occurrence a century ago, now uncommon by virtue of the advent of shoes and city sanitation ordinances) a kerosene-soaked rag. Ointments, too, were dependent on animal fat, herbs, and sweet oil. Amulets to ward off disease and remove symptoms are generally necklaces made of onions, garlic, asafetida (asfidity), various berries, magnets, iron filings; pennies, copper bracelets, and gold rings are worn often, and one remedy calls for drinking water in which gold or copper objects have soaked.

Magical transference and chants of exorcism are encountered rather frequently: A knife or pair of scissors placed under the bed or mattress "cuts" labor pains, that is, the pain is transferred to an associated object. A person with warts breaks up some sticks, places them in a brown paper bag, leaves the bag on a road and never looks back. Whoever picks up the bag gets the warts. Certain healers possess powers to remove warts, just as the mouth infection of infants, thrash [thrush], can be cured by a person born posthumously. A chant for burns reads:

> Ten little angels
> Coming from the North,
> One brought fire,
> One brought frost.
> Go out fire,
> Come in frost,
> In the name of the Father, the Son, and Holy Ghost.

The last line converts a primitive practice into a specifically Christian one.

Among the most interesting remedies are those involving vitamins and minerals necessary to the body's health, which were then un-

TREATING LICE

known or undefined. One tonic is a mixture of rhubarb and molasses—rhubarb is an excellent source of Vitamin C. Blood purifiers and strengtheners invariably involve iron: anvil dust, wagon dust, nails, poke salad, greens, raisins, and liver. A comic treatment for hiccups is: stand on your head and try to drink a glass of water. Onion juice and betsy bug blood are prescribed for earache, fat meat is applied to boils to burn out the poison, collard greens are literally stuck to the head for headache or one soaks his feet in a pan of water (whether to draw the pain from the head to the feet or simply to relax is not clear); for toothache, one may rub the jawbone of a hog over his face. The child with chicken pox is taken to the hen house where chickens are driven to fly over the head. Itch and sore-eyes are practically nonexistent today and snake bite is usually not fatal. But up until the '40s and '50s itch and head lice tormented the folk and snake bite was often certain death.

Since folk remedies are clearly related to the supernatural in certain aspects—magical transference, exorcism, talismans—there was very good argument for including them in the volume of sundry ghostly matters and superstitions. However, there is equally good argument for linking remedies with recipes. Behind them both stands the housewife. It is she who bakes the bread and staunches the nosebleed, who plucks the hen and concocts the brew, who gathers tomatoes, barks, roots, and herbs, who lays the table, applies the poultice, and administers cough syrup. In her single figure there are concentrated the disciplines and knowledge of generations. Mythically, she is giver and protector of life, healer and goddess of grains, fruits, and the young, beneficent and wise. And every day her energies and skills pour out upon her family, neighbors, and friends. Moreover, folk remedies resemble recipes in the listing of ingredients and in directions for composition and use. Finally, the very stuff and substance of remedies, save for a few drugs and those that require magic or conjurers, is the ordinary—the everyday items found in a nineteenth-century household and kitchen garden, indigenous plants, domesticated animals. The ingredients of remedies are often those of recipes—herbs like sassafras and ginger, onions, honey, vinegar, raw potatoes, hog lard, butter, chicken parts, eggs, tea. To be fair, it must be admitted that some herb doctors and conjurers were male, and husbands knew remedies quite as well as their wives; but as a general rule it was the woman who possessed the secrets of folk remedies, devised and administered medicines and cures, and nursed the sick. One is amazed at her good sense and ingenuity.

For convenience, folklorists sometimes separate remedies from superstitions. While this division is useful, we do well to remember that the principles of myth, magic, astrology, and witchcraft operate similarly in both areas. The more inclusive term "folk medicine" is often used as a designation for the aspect of folklore that deals not only with remedies per se but also with exorcism, the laying on of spells or conjuring, and healing by certain ill-defined psychic powers. Field investigations in the folk medicine of a particular culture are often reported in folklore journals. Collections of remedies exist in various folk archives, but rarely are they made available to the general reader. Tom Waller and Gene Killion have published a selection of folk remedies from the folklore papers housed in the Special Collections Department of the University of Georgia (*Southern Folklore Quarterly*, XXXVI, March, 1972) that are, as one might expect, similar to the ones in this volume. Occasionally, one finds a report of current wide-scale collection such as that cited by John Q. Anderson in his essay "Special Powers in Folk Cures and Remedies" (in *Tire Shrinker to Dragster*, Austin: University of Texas Press, 1968), a discussion of the stopping of blood and curing of warts and of screwworms in cattle by certain healers, seventh sons and daughters, and children born of deceased fathers. Mr. Anderson says that his folklore students at Teaxs A & M collected over six thousand remedies and placed them in the Texas Folk Archives.

The University of Texas has been, of course, a leader in folklore research since the days of J. Frank Dobie and Mody Boatwright. Though the scope of the Texas effort is national, even international, its greatest achievement has perhaps been the preservation and dissemination of the folklore of the Southwest, including the considerable Spanish-Mexican influence. One of the Texas folklore publications deserves special notice here for its comprehensive approach—*Tales From the Big Thicket* (ed. by Francis E. Albernathy; Austin: University of Texas Press, 1966) examines a definite geography in terms of its history and entire folk culture, customs, tales, songs, humor, and ancedotes. Interviews with local residents not only serve as the actual method of collection but provide extended examples of folk speech patterns. Now that folklorists have access to cameras and tape recorders, the interview is a significant factor in collecting and in the methodology of folklore research. Cecil Sharp's collection of over six hundred folksongs becomes the more remarkable when one considers that his only resources consisted of a notebook, a pencil, and a keen ear. The comprehensive approach to collecting folklore allows us to view the *whole*, to study, for example, the superstitions of a certain locality against the landscape of an entire community, to discern relationships between folk recipes and remedies and existing geography, botany, and agriculture, to study the origins of a ballad or song in some local event of history, and, simultaneously, to record a folk heritage in the living speech of the folk themselves. Such is one of the strengths of *Foxfire*.

Our own collection of remedies shares certain shortcomings, because of the limitations of its collectors, with many other collections. Although a list of remedies is valuable in and of itself for archivists, collectors, and general readers, it is immensely enlivened and more completely understood when the informant or teller himself speaks to us, when the teller has a name, a community, a sense of place, when he is, in actuality, a part of a folk culture. The comprehensive method is narrow, true, but this defect may be mended by comparative studies.

While our student collectors were not equipped to develop a comprehensive study of these Alabama folk remedies, they did manage in many instances to record actual speech or catch the flavor, rime, and syntactical and grammatical patterns of their informants. A few remedies were written out for the collector like a cookbook recipe; most written remedies were rendered with the directness and simplicity of an experienced cook. As with recipes, the apprentice healer learned by observation and participation. As with the recipes, the remedies are given essentially in the form in which they were taken down from the folk; and this necessarily involves some irregularity in spelling, grammar, and syntax. These brief verbalizations are a kind of short-hand for processes that were often eleborate, lengthy, and tedious. And, as with all medicines and curative treatments, healing lay in the heart as much as in the hand. Where diligence and faith and love could prevail, they did—victory over disease is ever sweet. When all reme-dies, skills, and love fell before the stings of death, there was left the kind of grief expressed in an epitaph we found on the small marble tombstone of a child: "If Love could have kept her, she would not be sleeping."

The publication of several books on nutrition, diet, and health prac-tices has stimulated a great national interest in home remedies. Unfor-tunately, a good many of the folk have followed the remedies to the exclusion of licensed doctors and medicine and have suffered the consequences. Quacks and faith healers still abuse their fellowmen with remedies that are often harmful and, at best, useless. Health foods, foods grown and processed without chemical additives, and organic gardening, though widely abused by misinformed zealots and exploited by those seeking commercial profit, are another indication of our interest in the folkways of another century.

The editors *do not* recommend that you experiment with the folk remedies that follow, however, sensible they may appear. They are presented as folklore, not as serious medicine. *We issue a clear, definite warning against these prescriptions.* If you happen to use them already, that is your business. Even if you do, consult your physician, not us or the contributors. Readers who are interested in the supernatural as-pect of remedies will want to look at another volume in this series, under superstitions. Scholarly studies of popular beliefs, folk medi-cine, and remedies are indexed in the bibliographical issues of *South-ern Folklore Quarterly.* An especially fine Alabama collection is Ray B. Browne's *Popular Beliefs and Practices from Alabama.* (Berkeley: Uni-versity of California Press, 1958).

Nose Bleed

String red corn like a necklace and put it around your neck to keep your nose from bleeding.

Mrs. Josie Blackwell

Put a piece of brown paper in the roof of your mouth to stop your nose from bleeding.

Mrs. Ora Lee Lawrence

In order to stop blood from the nose, beat up lead and hang this around the person's neck.

Mrs. Everett Russell

Take a dime and press it in the roof of mouth.
Place a pair of scissors down back of person whose nose is bleeding.

Mrs. Nadine McCall

If your nose is bleeding, let nine drops fall on a knife and stick it into the ground, and when it dries it will stop bleeding.

Theda Maughon

Soot and cobwebs stop bleeding.

Mrs. W. R. Harvey

Snuffing up powdered alum will generally control troublesome bleeding from the nose.
Place a wad of paper in the mouth of the person suffering from nose bleed. Instruct them to chew hard.
A nose bleed is frequently nature's way of relieving itself. If the bleeding continues, press the nose firmly between the finger and thumb for a few minutes. If this does not work, bathe the nose, forehead and nape of the neck with water quite cold from the well.
Hang pot hooks around the neck.
My grandfather can stop nosebleed by quoting a Bible verse. The only way to pass this verse on to someone else and keep his ability is to tell a woman of no relation. She in turn can tell a man of no relation.
My grandfather will not discuss this ability with me. The only way I found out about it was through his children. He declares he stopped my grandmother's nosebleed once.

Lois Campbell

Warts

Go out on a full moon and watch or concentrate on the glowing moon and say, "What I see glows, what I rub goes." Repeat this for three times for every night of that full moon and wart will disappear. You mustn't get confused though and say, "What I rub grows, what I see glows," or a curse will be put on yourself and the wart will become much larger.

Ann Johnson

To remove a wart break a red brick and rub the wart, then put the crumbled pieces in a package. The person who picks it up wil get the wart.

Mrs. Lee Stanford

To make warts go away, strike a match and pass the lighted match over them several times.

To get rid of warts place as many rocks in a brown paper sack as you have warts. Leave this sack on a dirt road, hide and watch to see if anybody picks up the sack. If they do, then your warts will go away, and the person who has the sack will get your warts.

Mr. E. C. Brooks

If a person has warts on his hands he can remove them by filling a match box with straws and dropping it in the road. If someone picks the box up and tries to use the straws, then the warts will disappear at this time.

Helen Massey

A good way to get rid of warts is to rub your wart with a chicken bone and then hide the bone.

Joe Parker

If you have any warts, pick up a rock in the road. Rub the rock on the wart. Then, throw the rock backwards down the road. The person who picks up the rock will get the wart and yours will be gone.

Eleanor Lee

While you are walking in the woods, find a bone and say, "Good morning" or "good evening" (whichever it is), pick it up, rub the wart, lay it down the same way, walk on and never look back.

Paul Thomas

To make a wart go away, notch a persimmon tree branch, bury it, and don't look back.

Mrs. Lee Stanford

If you have warts, get a string and tie a knot in it for every wart you have. Take the string and tie it to some tree and not go back for six months and your warts will go away.

Nadine Fuller

Rub a wart with a half potato. Put the potato out of sight. When the potato dries up the wart will be dried up.

Kathryn Moore

Cut a potato into as many pieces as there are warts. Feed the slices of potatoes to a pig, and the warts will disappear.

Abby

To remove a wart, write a verse of Bible scripture, squeeze the wart until blood comes, put a drop of blood on the piece of paper, then throw the paper in the road, and the wart will disappear.

Lizzie Ellison

To remove a wart, cut it and get a drop of blood to put on a piece of corn. Feed it to the chickens and the wart will disappear.

Bob Jones

WART CURE

To cure a wart, go to the cemetery at midnight and get some water from the newest grave. (Rub on the wart).

Linda Peebles

Make as many notches in a board as you have warts. Bury the board under the doorsteps. All warts will come off.

Mrs. C. T. Livingston

Rub string bean leaves on warts to make them disappear.

Altha Thompson

Take a small piece of beef or a bean and rub on the wart, then bury it, and as meat or bean rots so will the wart. When the meat or bean is completely rotted the wart will be gone.

Helen Massey

Steal a dishrag out of the kitchen and rub the warts with it and bury it under the doorstep and forget about it and the warts will go away.

Anne M. Conner

Rub wart of another person with big toe. After a week or so it will go away.
   Take straight pin and wipe it around the wart. It will soon disappear.

Tatum Bedsole

You can sell warts. The people will give you some money, preferably silver. Then you put a bandage over wart, wait about two weeks, take the bandage off and the wart will be gone.

Lana Silverthorne

Certain people can buy warts for a penny. The person that is selling the warts must promise to never rub them or look at them again and they will go away.

Phillip Norman

To cure a wart, get a frog and cut off one of his legs. Rut it on the wart and then the wart will jump off.

Mrs. Kate Windham

To cure warts pour vinegar on the hinge of a door after seeing a shooting star. The wart will then drop off, like a star.

Nora Wooton

To get rid of a wart, boil a needle, stick it in the wart and let it stay a few minutes, and the wart will go away.

Annie Floyd

If you have a wart tie a piece of horse's hair around the wart and it'll go away.

If a dog has warts change his name and it'll go away.

Melynda Malloy

The seventh male child of a family is able to get rid of warts, stop bleeding, and cure any kind of rash.

Mr. Parks

Catch a grasshopper and let the fluid from its mouth drip onto the wart, and it will disappear.

Mrs. Ed Hall

Stings and Bites

Bind on baking soda, dampened with water.
    Mix common dirt with water to about the consistency of mud—apply to sting.
    Tobacco juice applied freely.

M. O. Rushing

Take the leaves of tomatoes, crush and bind on a bee or wasp sting, and it draws out the sting at once.

Joe Parker

For a wasp sting: Use tobacco chewed up on the sting.

Mr. John McGill

Hold pins in the mouth when an insect bites and the bites will not become infected.

Mary Glenn Merritt

To kill chiggers grease the affected parts with lard.

Pearl White

For chigger (or "red bug") bites use fried salty meat grease.

Pearl White

Take a hair from the dog that bites you to cure the bite.

Minnie Jackson

For ant bites apply tobacco juice.

Mr. Jeff Pickson

To keep ants away put some kerosene in the mop water.

Joe Parker

If mosquitoes are bad, take some wool rags and put them in a pan. Set them afire. They will smolder and smoke. The smoke will run the mosquitoes away.

Mrs. Joe Gibson

Ground Itch

Collard leaves is good for ground itch.

Altha Thompson

To cure ground itch wrap feet in rabbit tobacco.

Altha Thompson

Bathe in digo tea made from digo weed for ground itch. (indigo)

Sula Weed

To cure ground itch step in hot cow manure and stay in it until the manure cools.

Charles L. Price

Sweet milk and gun powder cure ground itch.

Grace Deal

Sweet milk and cuckle berries boiled together cure ground itch.

Grace Deal

Boil sasafrass (roots, dirt, and everything) for thirty minutes and it will cure ground itch.

Linda Peebles

Place toad stool powder between toes.

Gussie Ramsey

For an itch use a mixture of hog lard and sulfur on the infected area.

Sula Weed

Sulfur and hog lard mixed together will cure itch.

Altha Thompson

Nutmeg, sulfur, and butter when mixed together is good for an itch.

Altha Thompson

To stop itching pat baking soda on wood poison.

Murry Thompson

To stop itching of an insect bite place a snuff polus on bitten area.

Mrs. A. L. Fleming

Rub milk of magnesia on mad itch to cure it.

Altha Thompson

Mix sulfur and grease and spread on seven-year itch to cure it.

Mrs. Tom Farmer

Skin Eruptions

If you have a fever blister, kiss a red-headed boy and it will go away.

Ear wax cures fever blisters.

Minnie Jackson

If you see a fever worm, spit on it three times or you will have fever blisters all over your mouth.

Mrs. Eunice Gulbreth

For pimples of the face:
Make a brine of epsom salts and pat on the face with cotton and let it dry on before going to bed. Do this until the pimples are dried up.

To remove freckles wash the face daily with buttermilk.

Mr. George Dunn

If you have freckles on your face go down to the woods and find a stump that is filled with water and bathe your face. Turn around three times and walk away. Never look back and your freckles will stay in the water in the stump.

Mary Ellen Warren

When babies are chafed, get on old rotten pine log and break off small pieces and beat it up until it is very fine like powder and use on the chafed areas.

Mr. James R. Cope

For chapped hands, face and feet
Melt with gentle heat, two ounces of sweet oil of almonds, half an ounce of spermoceti and one drahm of white wax. When melted, remove from the stove and add an ounce of glycerine, and stir until the mixture is cold. The ointment can be scented with any perfume to suit the fancy. Keep in wide-necked bottle.

Taken from an old Columbus,
Ga. newspaper around 1880

For a good smooth complexion use chittling grease.

Mr. Rice Eason

Put the milk from milk weed on your face and it will clear it up.

Mary Alice Wasden

Rub caster oil on a sore and there will be no scar.

Altha Thompson

Make plasters from peach tree leaves, stir them in water, and put them on the sores from plursy.

Mrs. Sarah Johnson

Alder tea is good for the blood; it cures sores.

Mrs. Lee Stanford

For an affected place on your hand take turpentine and beef tallow for it.

Mrs. Edna Windham

Mix together linseed oil, sweet gum, and tallow and apply as a salve to body sores.

Mrs. Jim Goff

To cure boils, make a poultice of goose manure and apply.

Mrs. Vassie Reeder

Eat raisins to get rid of boils.

Mrs. Jane Petrey

Onion polus for a boil.

Sula Weed

For risons or boils take white skin in the egg shell and place on it. This draws out the core and it will go away.

Biddie Lee

Risen or Carbuncle
Cut a pine tree. Let the fresh turpentine run out. Take the fresh turpentine mix it with tallow making salve. Spread a coat of the mixture on a cloth. Place it on the risen and it will draw it to a head.

Mrs. Malzie Metcalf

Boils
Take about a teacupful of the inside bark of birch and boil it in a quart of water. Boil it for a few minutes then drink this in place of water.

Joe Parker

Take one poke berry every morning for nine mornings for risens.

Mrs. "Murt" Strength

Sulphur and cream of tartar is a good blood purifer and will cure a "risen."

Mrs. Charles L. Price

For boils or risens take a bar of soap, meat or egg skin to make them come to a head.

Mrs. Margaret Crittenden

Place soap on a risen to cause it to run.

Altha Thompson

A mush polus of corn meal and water to bring risen to head.

Mrs. A. L. Fleming

Go to the blacksmith's shop and get some water where they have cooled their irons in it and drink the water for risens and carbuncles.

Mr. James H. Ham

For risings, use one tablespoon Octagon soap, three drops of turpentine, one teaspoon sugar, mix this together well, and put on rising. It will soon draw the infection to the surface.

Mrs. A. B. Gantt

Risen:
Put soap and sugar on a risen to make it come to a head. This keeps the risen from being sore and cures it.

Ginny Horne

Sometimes you will have a kernel on your body caused from a sore or infection. If you will go to a wash pot and make a cross on your kernel with the smut from the pot it will go away.

Jackie Kinsauld

If baby starts to smile but frowns, he is hivey.

Mr. W. F. Metcalf

For hives take a nine-day old child, prick his back, get a drop of blood and feed it to the child.

Mr. W. F. Metcalf

For baby hives
Take catnip leaves and put in cup.
Pour boiling water
Let steep—strain and add small amount of sugar.

Ola Bell Brooks

Cherry tree bark and whiskey is good for baby hives.

Mrs. Emmie Prestwood

Roast an onion in the fireplace and give a small baby the juice to break out the hives.

Mrs. Emmie Prestwood

Alum in shoes will kill the pain caused by corns.

Altha Thompson

Mix smoothly together a teaspoonful of pulverized indigo and the same quantity of brown soap and mutton suet. Spread on a piece of kid, and apply to the corn.

Effie Chestnut

Steal a small piece of beef. Bury it and as the meat rots the corn will go away.

Hattie Hall

Take a small onion, peel it, then take about a half a teacupful of strong vinegar and soak the onion on it for eight hours. Before going to bed take the inside of the onion and bind it on corns on the toes. When you get up the corn will be gone.

Joe Parker

Mumps

Make a halter and place over the patient's head. Lead him to a spring and make him drink water out of the spring.

Gussie Ramsey

Salt meat cures mumps.

Estella Freeman

Use the grease from hog jowl to cure the mumps.

Ruby Broyant

Take oil out of sardines and rub on jaws for mumps.

Miss Sara Doris Gilbert

My father would save hog jaw bones and lay them up. If anybody had mumps they would get the marrow out of the bones. They rubbed the person with the mumps on the jaw with the marrow.

Mrs. Maggie King

If you tie a string around your neck when you have the mumps, they won't fall on you.

Geral Dansby

Taste vinegar; if it stings, you have the mumps.

Mrs. Jeff Pickson

Measles

Take sheep pills and boil. Strain, make a tea, sweeten with sugar. Drink a cup full. That will break the measles out on a person good.

Mrs. W. R. Darman

Take some sassafrass roots and boil them. Sweeten the tea to taste. This is good for the measles. It will make them break out. This tea will purify the blood. Take a little each day.

Mrs. Ella Bundy

Take some sheep manure and pour water over it. Drain the water off and drink. It will make the measles break out.

Reverend George Gay

If you have measles and they won't come out, go out and stick your head in the chicken house and they will come out.

Mary Alice Wasden

To make measles pop out boil corn shucks and have the patient drink the tea.

Gussie Ramsey

Drink ginger tea to bring out measles.

Mrs. A. L. Fleming

Boil some shuck tea and drink it or boil some notebook paper and the ink from the lines on the paper will help break out with the measles faster.

Ada Cameron Cope

To make the measles or smallpox break out drink gin tea.

Mrs. Zack Crittenden

Drink hot tea made from whiskey and lemon juice to break measles out.

Annie Mae Locklar

Chicken Pox

Kill a chicken and scald him in some water. Then bathe the sick person in the water the chicken was scalded in.

Mrs. Clyde Harris

To cure chicken pox on children take them out to the chicken house at sundown and make the chickens fly out over them.

Mammie Fondern

Take chicken droppings and make a tea and give it to the sick person to drink.

Mrs. D. D. Parramore

Kill a chicken and bathe the sores with the chicken's blood and some water.

Mrs. Codie Windham

Kill a black chicken and drop its warm blood on the sores.

Mrs. Vassie Reeder

Sassafras tea is good to drink for the chicken pox.

Mrs. Lee Stanford

Worms

To cure worms in children, take Jerusalem seeds, boil them, mix with syrup and make into a candy and let the children eat it.

Mrs. Mae Reeves

A cure for worms in babies is the sack of asafetida tied around their neck. It is supposed to smell so bad that when the worms in the baby start going towards its head, they smell it and turn around and pass out.

Josephine Knight

Ring Worms
Rub the spot with milk from milkweed, which grows wild. Continue this a few days and the spot will disappear, or use nicotine from old pipe.

Mrs. Willard Grey

Have a Negro to mark a cross over the end with a piece of tallow.

Mrs. A. D. Watkins

Tape Worms

If a person has a tape worm, starve the person for several days. Then give a laxative to work him out good. Take pumpkin seeds and boil them and make a tea. Give a little of this to the patient. Have some one watch the patient's mouth. The tape worm will crawl up to his mouth. Grab his head and pinch it off. The rest of the worm will dry up and die. Then it will pass through the person.

Mrs. Bob Brackin

Hook Worms

Put tar in the gourd and drink water from it to keep down typhoid fever and hook worm.

Mr. George Grace

Kidney Worms

Roll ½ teaspoon of epsom salts until it is a fine powder, dissolve it in 1 teaspoon of syrup. Give this amount to a child about 3 or 4 hours before bed time and give him 2 tablespoons of milk of magnesia before breakfast—increase the amounts for older children—do not give any greasy food until the next day.

Fannie Cargile

Stomach Worms

Dip finger into turpentine and rub around the navel 3 times. This is good for stomach worms.

Mrs. Ola Cobb

Teething

3 doodle bugs in a cloth around neck. It will enable baby to cut teeth easily.

Lily Smith

To keep a baby healthy while it is teething, tie a cricket's nest in a rag put it around the baby's neck.

Sidney Taylor
and
Belle Wilkins

Put nine wood lice around your baby's neck and it will cut teeth easier.

Maylene Gavin

For cutting teeth hang tread salve roots or horse nettle around baby's neck. This will ease the pain of cutting the teeth.

Mrs. Frank Money

To make a baby cut teeth easier, kill a rabbit and take the brains while they are still warm, and rub the baby's gums. He won't have any trouble cutting teeth.

Mrs. J. C. Hudson

Rub a baby's gum with fur to make him cut his teeth quicker and easier.

Leo Roberts

Make a bag out of white clothes. Put seven folds in it. In the white bag put nine red ants. The baby will teeth easy without gums being sore.

Lucie Mae Black

Drive a hole in a penny and string it around the baby's neck with the penny resting in the sink of the baby's throat. You won't even know when the baby's teeth come through.

Take baby to a running branch and catch a live minnow. Rub babies gums with the minnow and throw him (minnow) back in the branch and watch him swim away.

Mrs. Lois Horath

Get a mole's foot for the baby to wear around its neck.

Mrs. J. C. Hickman

For Baby's Rest (Sleep)
1 medium size onion, unpeeled
1 wet cloth
Roast in stove oven or hot ashes until onion is soft. When removed, split in half, put 1 pinch of sulphur, place in clean cloth and squeeze juice for seasonings. Give 1 Tablespoon for rest.

Ola Bell Brooks

For Baby's Nerves
2 blocks of asphedia, pinch up tiny.
Put in pint bottle and fill with strong whiskey.
This will make the baby sleep.

Vicie Bentley

Thrash (Thrush)

Take a piece of cloth, put turpentine on cloth, rub it around in the child's mouth and stick it up the chimney. Do this for three mornings.

Let a Negro woman who has never seen her father, blow her breath in the child's mouth.

Mrs. Frank Money

Get some cottonwood leaves and wipe them around the person's mouth. This will cure the thrash for sure.

Mrs. Codie Windham

Take powdered alum and some honey, mix them together, and apply to the person's mouth.

Mrs. Jim Goff

If a baby has thrash, wipe his mouth with a white sheet and he will get well.

Elaine Lawrence

If a doctor cures thrash it will come back, and if it is conjured away it will never come back.

Mrs. Vassie Reeder

One may be cured of the thrash only if the one giving treatment has never seen his or her father. The most common cure seems to be the one of blowing in the baby's mouth.

Another is to rub a raw egg in the baby's mouth the first time you take him out.

Thrash may also be cured by taking some grease from a dirty skillet by rubbing your finger down the skillet and rubbing the finger in the baby's mouth.

Mr. Ervin Livingston, deceased, who lived in Dothan, Alabama, was able to cure the thrash in babies. He was unable to tell how this healing was done to anyone but one woman, who was not related to him. The woman, in turn, could tell one man who was not related to her.

Sylvia White

Sties

Rub a gold ring on eye for stys [sties] and they will go away.

Mrs. Maggie Hullen

Rub the sty nine times with a gold wedding band, that belongs to someone else. (Not your own)

Fannie Cargile

Go to a crossroads and say:
Sty, sty, leave my eye
Go to the next one passing by.

Mrs. A. D. Watkins

Take chicken manure and rub on a sty to make it come to a head and get well.

Cynthy Boone

If a man has a sty and a red-headed woman kisses him, it will go away.

Mrs. Ora Lee Lawrence

Get the dew off collard leaves early in the morning and use this for sore eyes. Put a drop of dew in each eye, and wipe your eyes with a cloth dipped in the dew.

Mrs. J. C. Hudson

Rub some of the first frost of the year on your eyes to ward off sore eyes.

Minnie Jackson

A mixture of yellow root tea and water to bathe sore eyes is a sure cure.

Friendly Roberson

To cure sore eyes boil lemon rind and then bathe eyes with the lemon rind tea.

Friendly Roberson

To cure the sore eyes bathe them with the first rain water of May.

Lorine McLendon

Take a cotton leaf when it has dew on it. Squeeze it and let the dew fall into the sore eye. It will be cured shortly.

Sidney Taylor
and
Cleatus Taylor

A green collard leaf heated in the oven and held over the eyes will cure sore eyes.

Maye P. Norris
and
Mrs. Lawrence McGowan

Use the cream off cow's milk to get gnats out of your eyes.

Mae Phillips

Use flax seed in the eye to bring out foreign matter.

Minnie Jackson

Colic

Take the root of a balsam plant and cut cross grain in small pieces. Cover the root with whiskey, give the baby 2 or 3 drops in milk. You may store and keep this on and on.

Mrs. Malzie Metcalf

Apply hot flannel wrung of hot water, also a foot bath.

Mrs. J. M. Moore

To cure baby's of colic give them briar root tea.

Mrs. A. L. Fleming

If a baby has the colic, it should be taken and placed in a chimney feet first with the head hanging down. Hold there for a few minutes. When the baby is taken down, the colic will be gone.

Friendly Roberson

Use asafoedity and whiskey for the colic.

Mrs. Lola Drake

Chew calamus roots, or put them in whiskey and drink only when needed.

Mrs. H. C. Cox

Rub their stomach with turpentine.

Mr. L. L. Strength

For the colic: Pour whiskey in a spoon and set fire. Burn the alcohol out and give to the baby.

Terry Coker

Grind beetles up and give the powdered beetles to the baby for the colic.

Minnie Jackson

Childbirth Pain

To ease labor pains:
The husband must go to a Holly Tree on the north side, reach as high as he can above his head and pick three limbs. Carry them back to the house and let someone take three limbs from those three and make tea from them for the wife to drink.

Clara Cassady

A sharp knife placed under a woman's bed makes her labor pains less.

Estella Freeman

Remedy for afterbirth pains:
Soon as the baby is born, place a pair of open scissors between the mattresses on patient's bed. These scissors will cut the pains.

Mrs. Elizabeth Donaldson

To lessen childbirth pain drink black pepper tea.

Biddie Lee

Epileptic Fits

Get a buck's horn, saw 12 pieces, each piece one inch long. Lay it in a frying pan and heat it until it has burned to ashes. Then pour it in a quart bottle, fill it with water. Give a teaspoon three times a day.

Penny Belcher

If a baby has epileptic fits near the fire place, take off part of his clothes and throw them in the fire and he will be cured.

Mrs. Mary Coleman

Wearing a piece of asafetida tied around the neck will keep off spells.

Old folk remedy

Cook some onions and put a piece of cloth large enough to tie around the pulse or your wrist into the juice of the onion and tie to the wrist. (You may want to add some onion in the cloth)

Ada Cameron Cope

In convulsions of children, to turn them upon their left side will cut short, like magic, the convulsions. Epileptics treated in the same way are always promptly relieved.

Mrs. Willard Grey

Cancer

If you have cancer, eat plenty of figs.

Mrs. Florine Metcalf

Put the clay in the stove and bake it. Some have quit eating it because it causes cancer and makes things grow in one's entrails.

Rose Reynolds

They say that a person who eats onions will never have cancer.

Lois S. Harris

Take the dried blossoms of the common red clover, put them in hot water, let them steep over night and this will be clover tea. Take a tablespoonful of this tea five or six times a day. Cases of virulent cancer have been cured by this simple remedy.

I know an old lady that cured herself of a cancer in the face by making a strong tea of red clover flowers, and drinking it all the time and rubbing it on the bump too. It went down to the size of a bean and finally dropped off.

This cured my mother of a cancer which she had on her arm and it had began to eat and would take spells bleeding. A friend told her to get Witch Hazel and boil it down to a strong tea, strain and then take pure hog's lard and make a salve with the tea and lard. It sure cured her arm. She took a white cloth, and spread a small quantity of this salve on, and bound it to her arm once a day and it cured her sound and well and there was no sign of it ever coming back.

Donor Unnamed

Hiccups

Put a big brown paper bag over your head. Leave it there until the hiccups stop, it won't be long.

Mrs. O. L. Thaggard, Sr.

Some persons still believe swallowing a teaspoonful of sugar stops hiccups.

Floy Parmer

To cure a baby of hiccups put a straw in her hair.

Naomi

Look up and say 14 times:
Look up and I won't hiccup.

Elaine Lawrence

To stop hiccups, drink a gallon of water.

Eunice Gulbreth

Nine swallows of water will stop the hiccups.

Mrs. Lewis Newton

To get rid of hiccups swallow a teaspoonful of sugar.
    Some advice to hiccups victims, stand on your head and try to drink a glass of water.

Kidney, Bladder Trouble

For kidney, bladder and prostate gland trouble:
Soak pine needles in water for three or four days and drink the water.

Mattie Goodson

Corn silk is good for kidney trouble.

Jimmie Sue Phillips

Drink epsom mixed in water to cure kidney infection.

Altha Thompson

To take a little ball of pine rawsum is good for kidney trouble.

Altha Thompson

Watermelon seed tea will cure bladder trouble.

Lena Tatum

Take 1 tablespoon of swamp root before each meal. This will allow the kidneys to function properly.

Vicie Bentley

For a kidney ailment boil bear grass and take the tea and drink it as often as desired.

Mrs. Everett Russell

Parch egg shells and pour water over this to make a tea. Drink this for kidney ailment.

Mrs. Everett Russell

For any kidney ailment boil red oak bark and drink the tea.

Mrs. Everett Russell

Bowel Trouble

Take one pomegranate and boil it. Take the tea from the boiled pomegranate hulls and give it to a child or an adult with diarrhea.

Mrs. Nellis Garret

For diarrhea take a little bark off the north side of a red oak tree. Get as much as you can hold in your hand. Boil some water and let water get cold and then put bark in the water and drink it.

Mrs. J. M. Thompson

Boil roots of Runner Oaks and give it hot for loose bowels.

Bennie Frank Smith

If your bowels are upset put some slack lime in a jar of water and drink it. This will cure you of your problem.

Mrs. Jim Goff

Drink blackberry root tea for bowel trouble.

Sula Weed

For bile trouble when I was a youngen we would kill a chicken and get the skin off the gizzard and boil it and give tea off it.

Mrs. W. H. McMurray

Gather blue graze roots, boil them into a tea and drink the tea as a laxative.

Mrs. Sarah Johnson

Rub a baby's navel with castor oil to make its bowels move.

Nan Hanson

Roll blue mash into balls and then roll in soda. Give one pill size of okra seed for three nights. Skip three nights. Give for three nights. Skip three nights. And give for three more nights. Nine pills in all. Then give castor oil to clean out system.

Mrs. W. H. McMurray

Blood Purifiers

To purify your blood put some tar in a bucket of cedar water and drink the drained-off liquid.

Mrs. Alice Holloway

When a red shank root is boiled in water, drink this to purify the blood.

Mr. Mac Amos

Drink sassafras tea to purify the blood.

Miss Sallie Mae Foy

Take the leaves of a Poke bush, make them into a salad. When this is eaten, it will put double iron in the blood. It makes a long life.

Mr. Mac Amos

Anvil dust is good for iron in the blood.

J. A. Rinhart

If you drink wine it makes you have rich blood.

Geral Dansby

Eat liver and rasins and you will get rid of your bad blood.

Glenda Eddings

For Blood Poison
1½ pints kerosene
1 oz. iodine
2 oz. camphor gum

Mix all together

J. A. Rinhart

Spring Tonics

Wash sasafrass roots well. Cover with water and simmer while cooking dinner. Serve hot with sugar if desired.

W. B. Gantt

Put a gold dollar into a jar of water and then drink the water. This will give a person good health.

Mrs. Carola Windham

Take the bark from a red oak tree, boil, and make a tonic. It is good for both humans and animals.

Mr. Zack Crittenden

If you were a puny person who didn't have any appetite you would take some rusty nails, put them in a bottle of vinegar, and let the bottle stand over night. Then drink the solution. This will make you healthful again.

Mrs. Jim Goff

Gather some fever grass and put it in a bottle of vinegar with some rusty nails in it and take as a spring tonic.

Mrs. Alice Holloway

Put a handful of rusty nails in a quart jar. Fill the jar with vinegar. Give a tablespoon three times a day to puny children.

Mrs. Joe McNeill

Mix Blue Moss with some calomine. Make pills out of this. Take 2 pills about 30 minutes apart. In the morning take a big dose of castor oil. This was given to the children every spring.

Mrs. Joe McNeill

File off some of the iron rim of the wagon wheel. It will be almost powder. Take a pinch daily. This is a good tonic to build you up.

Mr. M. M. Chestnut

Take some mullin leaves and boil them. Drain the water off and take as a spring tonic.

Reverend George Gay

Go to branch and get some Alder. Break it up into pieces and put the sticks in a fruit jar and cover with branch water. Drink as needed at springtime. That's the best Spring Tonic there ever was!

Mrs. J. A. Godwin

Boil rhubarb and molasses together. This makes a good spring tonic. Take a teaspoon every day.

Mrs. Joe Gibson

May rain water was considered healthy and all the children were made to get out in first May rain.

Mrs. Fannie Sanders

Winter Ailments Cured
Take the tender shoots and leaves of polk weed. Wash and cook like young turnips.

Snap bamboo shoots like string beans. Cook and season like beans. This gets vitamins into the system.

Eva Gantt

Tonic Drink
A quarter of an ounce of camomile flowers;
A quarter of an ounce of sliced gentian root;
A quarter of an ounce of bruised columba;
A quarter of an ounce of dried orange peel;
Fifty cloves bruised; a pint and a quarter of cold spring water.

Put these ingredients into a jug, and pour on them rather more than a pint of cold spring water; let it stand twenty-four hours, then pour off clear liquor. Take three tablespoonfuls for a dose, fasting every morning.

Mrs. Sula Pridgen

Rheumatism

Wear a gold ring on the middle finger of the right hand to cure rheumatism.

Altha Thompson

Five cents worth of nitre potassium, twenty cents worth of iodide potassium in one pint of water. Take one tablespoon three times a day before each meal. If followed as directed will cure rheumatism without fail.

Mrs. Willard Grey

Grancer Grey Beard and Whiskey for Rheumatism.

Eva Yarbrough

A mixture of cedar buds and white gas is good for rheumatism.

Altha Thompson

Buckeye balls carried in pocket is good for rheumatism.

Sula Weed

Use magnets to draw rheumatism out of the body.

Minnie Jackson

Tie a dime around the ankle to keep rheumatism away.

Leah Ivey

To cure rheumatism let bees sting you.

Mrs. Mary Hammock

To cure rheumatism eat some polk berries.

Mrs. Addie Mathison

Get a pint of whiskey, put some moth balls in it and add a little terpentine, vinegar, and white whiskey. Rub this solution on your rheumatic sores.

Mrs. Coddie Windham

NETTING BUZZARD

For rheumatic pains take and eat some yellow dock roots.

Mrs. Zuleika McCleod

Arthritis

Copper nails worn in the shoes were once thought to ground the pain of arthritis.

A copper penny or wire tied around the diseased limb will cure arthritis.

Johnnie Woodham

Apple Cider Vinegar plus pure honey yields a mixture that is a cure for arthritis.

Mrs. A. L. Fleming

To cure arthritis take white ash bark and beat it up, and then mix this with whiskey.

Mrs. Everett Russell

Measure one half cup of table salt and put into pint bottle. Finishing filling bottle with gasoline. Apply this liquid to aching joints.

Mrs. W. H. Williamson

Sprains, Bruises, Soreness, Swelling

Boil a buzzard gizzard, add some lard and stew, then rub on aching muscles.

James R. Cope

Get a handfull of clay and mix it with a spoonful of vinegar. Put this on the sprain.

Don Dixon
and
Mrs. Willie Shiver

If you sprain your foot, go to a branch where the water is running freely and let your foot stay in it for a good little while.

Cynthy Boone

Take cow manure and put it on a sprained muscle and let it stay for awhile.

Fostelle Dixon

SPRAIN MEDICINE

For "sprang" ankle wrap it in a polus of clay and moss from a spring mixed with vinegar.

Sula Weed

Mullein leaves dipped into boiling water, good to relieve swollen joints, sprains, and muscle strains.

Mrs. Mary Elizabeth Yeargan

Take popgun elder, scrap it, and then boil it. Drink the tea from this to make the swelling go down.

Mrs. Gus Cheatham

Heat salt in oven to relieve joint pains and aches.

Mrs. Lois Throyer

½ cup of table salt—put in a pint bottle, fill with gasoline. The salt will not dissolve. Shake well before applying to aching joints.

M. O. Rushing

Mix sweet oil and laudanum in equal quantities, and apply to the bruise. It will relieve the soreness and prevent discoloration.

Effie Chestnut

Put a slice of raw potato on a bruise to ease the pain.

Lamar Parker

Take raw cotton and roll into string. Wet in turpentine and tie around leg. This will eliminate cramp.

Ola Bell Brooks

Remedy for Sore Leg
Take ½ lb, perhaps ¼ lb. alum, a piece of blue stone the size of a pea, put it in a bottle and fill it with chamber lye—wash the sore with it. Salve 4-oz tallow, 4-oz of lard 2-ox bees wax, a tea cup full of spirits of turpentine, ¼ oz of campher, 1 hand full elder bark, 1 handful of hart leaves, 1 hand full heal-all, boil the herbs together until it becomes very strong; take out the herbs and put the liquor with the above mentioned and boil all together until the water is out then strain it, and then it is fit for use. July the 22th, 1849.

Faye Balkom

Neck Cricks
Pound up mullein leaves and mix with turpentine and kerosene. Put the poultice on your neck. Good for neck cricks.

Minnie Jackson

Go to a tree where hogs have rubbed after same have rolled in mud. Rub neck where hogs rubbed getting some of the mud where the crick is. Before the day ends Crick Is Gone!

Mrs. J. A. Godwin

High Blood Pressure

For high blood pressure, take mistletoe, dry it, put into a cup and pour hot water over it and drink as a tea.

Mrs. Kirby Kent

Calimus plant roots are used for high blood pressure.

Mr. Zack Crittenden

Boil and strain garlic seed. This is good for high blood pressure.

Mr. Mac Amos

To help high blood pressure, the hair is tied tightly in the top of the head, sometimes twisted with a match and the match lighted.

Louisa January

Leeches on the body will help high blood pressure.

Mrs. Eunice Gulbreth

Fever

Make a tea from fever grass and drink it for the fever.

Ruby Broyant

Get some fever grass and boil it. Use the tea to take, to make your fever come down.

Mr. M. M. Chestnutt

To break the fever: Get cherry bark, blacksnake root, whiskey, and rusty nails—put all of it together and boil it to make a tea. Drink the tea for the fever.

Mr. Gerald Pennington

A pan of water under the bed of a fever patient will drive away the fever.

Mary Glenn Merritt

To cure body heat, bathe in water that has been sunned for a good while.

Mrs. A. L. Fleming

To lower fever: Place turpentine in a saucer and put under the bed of the ill person.

Gussie Ramsey

Bind baking soda in a poltice to the pulse to cool a fever.

Murry Thompson

Put turpentine in boiling water and inhale for hay fever.

Mrs. J. M. Thompson

Malaria Fever

Use a small bunch of yellow tops. Wash yellow tops and boil in three quarts of water. You should have about a quart and a half of this mixture when it is ready. Strain. Cool. To this amount add three tablespoons of baking soda, to this mixture. Give the patient about a half small glass of liquid, and use the remaining mixture to rub on patient.

Mrs. Callie Knowles
and
Hattie Hill

We use to take Blue Gin for the malaria fever. It had quinine in it. It was very bitter and a bad dose of medicine.

Mrs. L. H. Franklin

For malaria fever gather alder bark, cherry bark, and dogwood bark, cut these up, put in a bottle of whiskey, and let it stand for several days. Then drink a swallow three times a day.

Mrs. Jim Goff

For malaria take some turpentine and some castor oil.

Mrs. Alice Holloway

Snake Bites

For a rattlesnake bite, give the victim as much pure hog's lard as he can take for 24 hours. Then after 24 hours are up from drinking the lard, give him as much sweet milk as he can drink.

A. B. Gantt

If one gets bitten by a green snake, he should take a black chicken, cut it open, and let the blood drip on the bite to kill the poison.

Mrs. Lee Stanford

For a snake bite, "Run, kill a black chicken, snap its head off, and quickly put the bleeding neck against the bite."

Mrs. Ruby Turner

If a snakes bites you, cut snake open and stick it to snake bite and this will draw poison out.

Terry Coker

Whiskey is good for snake bite.

H. L. Holman

Headache

Put salt on top of the head and tie a rag around it tight for the headache.

Nellis Garret

Catnip tea helps to cure headaches.

Mrs. Willie Raines

Fill a tub almost full of hot water. Put your feet in this and cover over with a quilt. Let your feet soak for about 30 minutes. Keep adding hot water. This will help a headache.

Mrs. J. C. Hudson

Salt put on the head is good for a headache.

Sula Weed

Headache.
To cure a simple headache immerse the feet in hot water, and keep them there for twenty minutes. If the pain is severe, add tablespoonful of dry mustard, keeping the water as hot as can be borne.
Sick Headache.
Two teaspoonfuls of finely powdered charcoal, dunk in half a tumbler of water, will often give relief when caused by superabundance of acid in the stomach.

Sam Price

Collard leaves tied around head will cure headache.

Friendly Roberson

Tie Canna leaves around your head to cure the headache.

Mrs. George Matthews, Jr.

Small Wounds

If you stick a nail in your foot, put a piece of fat meat on it to draw the poison out.

Ora Lee Lawrence

To take a splinter out of your foot or anyplace where you stick one in you, cut a piece of fat meat and bind it over the splinter. It will draw the splinter out by morning.

Mrs. Joe Hilson

If you have stuck a nail in your foot, soak it in kerosene.

Laura Turner

For nail stuck in foot, apply kerosene to keep blood poison down.

Mrs. A. D. Watkins

When you stick a nail in your foot, take some turpentine and add a little sugar to it. Bind this on the place where the nail stuck in.

Mrs. Pearl Clark

When you stick a nail in your foot wrap it in Castor Oil.

Grace Deal

If you stick a nail in your foot, smoke it with a burning wool hat.

Charles L. Price

When a person sticks a nail in his foot, make a fire from rags dipped in turpentine. The fire should be made in a can with just enough rags to make smoke. Put the place where the nail stuck in over the smoke. This will take out all the soreness.

Mrs. Clint Felts

If you stick a nail in your foot do this. Get some old wool rags and put them in a bucket; set them afire. It won't burn with a flame. It will smoke. Put your foot over the top of the bucket and cover it up with a quilt. Let it smoke for several hours.

Mrs. Joe McNiell

Fill an old bucket with pieces of woolen cloth, chicken feathers (other will do), and set fire. Let the foot stay over this smoke. This will keep the wound open and will help the pain.

Mrs. Robert Moore

If you stick a nail in your foot, take some oak wood ashes and dampen them with water. Bind this to the place where the nail stuck in.

Mrs. Joe McNeill

When you have a nail stuck in your foot get red oak bark and boil and make a poultice out of meal and salt. Put this poultice on the foot to draw out infection.

Mrs. Willie Threat

To treat a person who has stuck a nail in the foot, soak the foot for a long time in kerosene oil. Dry the foot off good. Then smoke the foot over an old bucket with woolen rags, which have been set afire, and have begun to smoke. This will help to avoid having blood poisoning.

Mrs. A. B. Gantt

Burns

Talking out Fire
Take patient in room by yourself and say the following:
"Two little angels coming from the North, one brought fire
one brought frost.
Go out fire.
Come in frost.
In the name of the Father, the Son and the Holy Ghost. Amen."

Mrs. Lois Horath

For a burn: Say to self and blow on burn:
Two Indians came from the North,
One brought frost, One brought fire,
Out fire with frost,
In the name of the Father, Son, and Holy Ghost.

Mrs. A. D. Watkins

To cool a burn put egg whites mixed with cooking oil on the burn.

Sula Weed

Mix sweet gum leaves and corn stalks (after they have dried out) with
syrup—smear on burns.

"Uncle" Charlie Smith

Use honey for skin burns. Relieves pain and prevents formation of
blisters.

The Rice Eason Family

Put syrup and soda on a grease burn.

Mrs. Louise Watson

Cream off of milk is good for sun burns.

Mrs. Arabelle Smith

Put vanilla flavoring on a burn.

Mrs. Bert W. Hattaway

For burns use machine oil.

Travis Marsh

Put wet baking soda on a burn.

Nadine Fuller

For burns and swelling: Scrape irish potato and make a poltice. Place on burned area or swollen area.

Mrs. Willie Shiver

Ink is good for a minor burn.

Sue Peacock

If a child gets into a pepper patch take him to the hen house—it will stop the burning and—make him sit——

Kate Hines

For sun burn
Mayonnaise, salad dressing or butter.

Mr. J. G. Presnell

Vinegar and soda mixed together into a paste and apply to blistered part.

Mrs. Eula Mae Hunley

Earache

For the ear ache, boil an onion in water and put a few drops of the onion juice in your ear.

Mrs. Mamie Pennington

To cure the ear ache, take a Betsy Bug, pull it in two, it has one drop of blood and put it in the ear. It will stop the ear ache.

Mr. L. V. Reeves

Pour boiled peach seed liquor into ear for ear ache.

Sula Weed

To cure an ear ache, heat a small sack of salt and put on ear.

Mrs. Willie Threat

Cure the ear ache by keeping the painful ear filled with goose grease.

Mr. Zack Crittenden

Take a large onion cut in the center, take the layers apart without breaking the thin skin between them, then sprinkle fine cut tobacco between the layers, put back together and roast. Take the juice from it, and put two drops in the ear.

Joe Parker

For ear ache put hot ashes into a bag—wet the bag and lay it on the ear. The hot steam will go down into the ear and cure the ear ache.

The Rice Eason family

Blow tobacco smoke in the ear for the ear ache.

Barbara Nichols

Toothache

Put hot sack of salt on place next to the tooth.

Mrs. Lum Bradley

Apply a bit of cotton—dampened in a solution of ammonia to the tooth. Usually relieves the pain almost immediately.

Hattie Hill

Use oil of cloves as linament for tooth ache.

Mrs. A. D. Watkins

If you have a tooth ache, dig up some prickley pear, scrape the roots of the bush and it will kill your tooth ache.

Theda Maughon

Take a hog jawbone and rub your face with it for the tooth ache.

Mrs. Helen Johnson

For the toothache mix Rooster snuff with water and then put it on the tooth that is hurting.

Lorine McLendon

When you have the tooth ache take green coffee until it is real strong and hold it on your tooth. By the time you use about a pint of this the ache will be gone.

Mrs. Nellie Birch

For the tooth ache mix camphor with turpentine. Then place the mixture on the hurting tooth.

Friendly Roberson

POULTICE

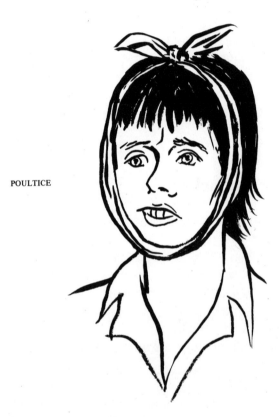

Boil meal and put in a bag for tooth ache and ear ache.

Mrs. W. H. McMurray

Upset Stomach

Crush and strip peach tree leaves. Drink water slowly. This is for vomiting.

Mrs. Sula Pridgen

Broiled chicken gizzard broth or charcoal broth are excellent to settle upset stomach.

Ruth Neely Parks

Butterfly root tea would cure upset stomach. (The butterfly weed is a small weed, has reddish orange blooms that sort of resemble a butterfly.) You boil the roots and strain the liquid and give in small amounts to drink.

Maye P. Norris

Soot is good for the stomach ache.

Mrs. Phil Williams

For stomach ache rub twelve circles of turpentine around the navel.

Nancy Matilda Geshagan

Take the bark from an Elm tree, chew and swallow for the stomach ache.

Mrs. Zack Crittenden

For a sick stomach take some queens delight, peal it and eat.

Mr. Zack Crittenden

If you have a sick stomach place a cold egg on your throat.

Lucille Motley

Sow bugs brewed in hot water and after drink the tea will cure the upset stomach.

Mr. Avery

Make a mustard plaster and put on stomach until it burns a little. This is good to settle the stomach.

Mrs. Willard Grey

Dig sampsons snake root out of ground. Cut roots into pieces. Put in bottle and add whiskey.

Ola Bell Brooks

Briar root tea is good for babies with stomach infection.

Altha Thompson

Boil charcoal and drink the water to cure an upset stomach.

Indigestion

1 quart boiled water
1 teaspoon epsom salts
½ teaspoon baking soda
1 small bottle peppermint drops

Mix together and keep in cool place. This is guaranteed to relieve indigestion.

Florence Taylor

Boil some snake roots and drink.

Mr. James Ruben Cope

If you have gas pains in your right side, reach down with your right hand and pick up a stick. Spit on the stick and throw it back behind you.

Mr. L. L. Strength

Pneumonia

Take six onions, fine chip, put into a large spider over a hot fire, add vinegar and rye meal to form a thick paste, stir and simmer ten minutes. Put into cotton bag large enough to cover the lungs, and apply as hot as the patient can bear. In about ten minutes change the poultice, continue reheating poultice. In a few hours the patient will be out of danger. But continue until perspiration starts freely from the chest. Make two poultices. Also an excellent remedy for croup when applied to the throat.

Mrs. Willard Grey

For pneumonia, make an onion polis, using meal to help hold it together. Place on the chest as warm as the patient can stand. Keep this up until the patient begins to get relief.

Mrs. A. B. Gantt

Drink fever grass tea to cure pneumonia.

Lorine McLendon

Boil pine needles in water. Use a sheet and make a tent. Place container under tent so vapor will fill the tent. This will reduce high fever.

Take one quart of cotton seeds and put in small bag or cloth and crush. Add to this one pint of corn meal, one cup salt, and about one-half cup soda. Mix this with hot water and place on clean cloth, or in a small bag, and put on the side and chest of sick person. Be sure the patient is covered well at all times.

To break a high fever make a strong tea from fresh cow manure. Put manure in water and boil,when cool let patient drink a small cupful every few hours.

Mix one half cup of tallow, one half cup tar (taken from fat pine wood), with a few drops of turpentine, fry over heat and place on a cloth. This applied to chest will reduce fever.

Mrs. Ola Cobb*

Take tallow and add Vick's salve, a few drops of kerosene, a few drops of turpentine and soak a cloth in it real good. Get it as hot as you can and put it on the chest and leave it on all night.

Mrs. Maye Price

Asthma

Gather green moss, make a pillow and let the one who has the asthma sleep on the moss pillow over night.

Mrs. Ruth Grimes

Bore a hole in door facing at the level of top of child's head. Cut lock of hair and stick it in the hole. Then drive a nail in the hole and when child grows above the hole he won't ever have asthma again.

Alice Darby

Place lard on flannel and sprinkle with black pepper then place on chest.

Pearl White

---

*Editor's Note: An elderly lady recently told us of wearing a "Tar Jacket" for a long siege of pneumonia during her childhood. She remembered vividly the discomfort of such a smelly encumbrance while she lay on a feather mattress in late spring!

A syrup made from the bark of wild plum is a sure cure for asthma. The syrup is made from steeping a handful of the bark of the plum in a quart of water. Boil down to a pint and add enough sugar to make a syrup.

Helen Massey

Bore a hole in a tree. Cut a lock of your hair and put it in the hole to cure asthma.

Minnie Jackson

Take Pinex and mix with honey and take one teaspoon morning and night for asthma.

Lucille Motley

To cure asthma catch a frog, hold it up to your mouth, open the frogs mouth and breathe in the frog's mouth three times. Put the frog down unharmed.

Mr. L. V. Reeves

To cure asthma take some Jimson weed leaves, dry them, break into small pieces and smoke it, inhale the smoke.

Mr. Zack Crittenden

Colds, Flu

For colds put tallow, terpentine, and kerosene into a searcloth and warm the cloth and then put in on your chest for your cold.

Mrs. Sarah Johnson

To keep off colds, take a Sweet Gum Ball from the tree, drop in a small bottle of Rum. Then take one tablespoon at night and in the morning during the winter.

Mrs. Maye Price

Put mullet leaves on a child's chest to help a cold.

Mrs. Dalton Thomley

To cure a common cold fever take Yellow Bods Roots, thread them on a string and then wear the string around the neck until the roots are dried up. When the roots are dried up the cold fever will be gone.

Friendly Roberson

Feed a cold and starve a fever. (Don't eat if you have a fever.)

Mrs. Pauline Allen

Wear the weed, yellow dot, to keep off cold.

Sula Weed

Grease a baby's legs with tallow to keep the colds off.

Leah Ivey

To cure a cold take axle grease, tallow and turpentine. Mix and spread on a rag and tie around the neck and body.

Mrs. Mae Reeves

Eat onions and sugar and you won't have a cold.

Floyd Sikes

For remedy for a cold take equal portions of honey, vinegar, castor oil, and butter, and heat them in a pan. Take a spoonful of this every time your child coughed.

Mrs. Zuleika McCleod

When a baby has a cold, grease the bottom of his feet with warm tallow, also his forehead and warm him before the fire. Place him in a warm bed.

Mrs. H. C. Cox

If you will wet your head the 1st rain in May, you won't catch cold from getting wet during the rest of the year.

Charles L. Price

Asphodity and whiskey prevent one from taking a cold.

Mrs. Everette Russell

Hold a piece of fat meat over a lightwood splinter. Let the smoky vapors fill the room. This will open the head when it is stuffed up.

Fannie Cargile

For a good cough syrup—mix a small amount of honey, apple cider, and vinegar.

Rub feet with tallow and bake them before an open fire.

Heat a small amount of camphor in water and inhale the fumes, this will relieve tightness in the head caused by colds.

Mix camphor, Vicks salve, possum oil, sweet oil, kerosene, tar and heat. Fry a cloth in this mixture and place on chest of the person having difficulty in breathing.

Mrs. Callie Knowles

Mix tar, camphor, Vicks salve, tallow, sweet oil, kerosene in an old frying pan and heat—"fry" a large cloth in this and pin it securely to the undershirt of the sick person.

M. O. Rushing

An old cure for head colds and congestions called for wearing necklace of wild onions for three successive days.

Mammie Fondern

Tar Jacket

Take tar, turpentine, grease, and tallow and mix it together. Wet a cloth in this and put it on your chest when you have a real bad chest cold or pain in your chest and it'll move it.

Sue Peacock

Bind bacon rinds around the neck for sore throats or tie soiled hose around the neck.

Minnie Jackson

For a cold eat honey because it is made out of wild flowers.

Eva Hayes

If you have a cold drink hot tea brewed from field balsom.

David Atkinson

Boil hog hooves in water and then drink the solution to cure a bad cold.

Mrs. A. L. Fleming

Take mully and pine top and rabbit tobacco. Boil. Put syrup in it for the flu.

Mrs. Johnny Holt

Chip up a bowl of fresh onions and put sugar over it. Eat this and go to bed and you will sweat the flu out of you.

Mr. Morris Hataway

Cure for flu: Make pig's hoof tea and drink it; or dry pig's foot and grind it up and drink it.

Tom Lovejoy

Cherry bark and whiskey are good for most any bad cold or flu.

Mrs. J. M. Thomspon

To prevent flu put one tablespoon of dry sulphur in each shoe.

Eulska Johnson

For flu:
Mix cow dung and pine tops in white rag and boil in coffee pot. Strain in another white rag and make tea. If you use sheep pills instead of the cow dung you can cure the measles over night.

Flu remedy
Boil in Pot, Hog's hoof, pine tal, oak bark, hog's tongue. After it has boiled for a while, then drink.

Otis Henry

Coughs, Croup

Whooping Cough
Take a turnip, the size of a hen egg, slice it up, make a syrup of sugar and water, and pour over the turnip while the sugar is warm. Let stand about an hour, and then take a teaspoonful every two hours. It is good for Whooping Cough.

Take piece of asafetida about the size of a nickel, set it on to a string and wear it around the neck.

Mrs. Ruth Grimes

I can tell you about a remedy we found to work in a case of whooping cough when our children were small. We placed thin slices of garlic in his shoes, fresh each day. This is a very simple remedy but we found that our child didn't suffer nearly as much as the children of our neighbor's who lauughed at what they called foolishness.

Nellie Parker

Whooping cough can be cured by feeding the child mare's milk.

Melynda Malloy

Dissolve 1 teaspoon of alum in ½ pint of honey. Give as needed for coughs.

Fannie Cargile

Catch a pole cat and kill it. Use the grease for rubbing body of patient.

Thelma Moody

Horse milk is good for the whooping cough. Sweet gum, honey, and tar cooked up together is good too for the whooping cough.

Mrs. Edd Horn

Drink Mullin tea for the whooping cough.

Mr. George Grace

Roll babies around in a hog pen to cure whooping cough.

Minnie Jackson

If a child has whooping cough catch a toad frog and hold it right close to the child's mouth so that the toad will catch the child's breath. Then take the frog to the fireplace and put it in a corner. It will whoop until it is dead and by that time the child's whooping cough will be gone.

Mrs. Nellie Birch

Wild mullen boiled with honey yields a mixture that will cure whooping cough.

Altha Thompson

Jay Bird soup if drank will cure whooping cough.

Sula Weed

Water out of a mule trough will cure the whooping cough.

Leah Ivy

If you don't change your name after marriage, then that person can chew a baby's food and feet it to him and also cure him of whooping cough if he has it.

Mrs. Carola Windham

Use allum, honey, baking soda, and lemon juice for whooping cough.

Mrs. Addie Mathison

Cough Remedy
1 Box of Pinix at drug store
½ teaspoon of it mix well with this then 3 times of honey
also:
1 big spoon of syrup
1 big spoon castor oil
1 big spoon Paragoric

Shake all well, then 3 times a day.

James Thomas

Old Fashioned Onion Cough Syrup
Boil several onions in about 1 quart of water until they are soft. Mash up and add enough sugar to make a thick syrup. Be sure all sugar is dissolved in hot liquid. Take as needed for cough.

Jack Miller

Take whiskey and Black Draught for coughs.

Mrs. Vassie Reeder

Mix honey and apple cider vinegar for coughs due to colds.

Fannie Cargile

For a cough drink hot tea made by boiling mullen leaves and hoar hounds.

David Atkinson

Croup
Burn a fat pine splinter and hold salt pork over it and allow the drippings to fall on the fire and let the child inhale the fumes for the croup.

Mrs. Mamie Pennington
and
Mrs. Vassie Reeder

For croup mix a teaspoon of honey and soda.

June Parker

I have always heard to cure the croup, you should take a child out in the yard and stand him on the ground barefooted.

Mrs. Gene Myers

Saturate a piece of flannel in turpentine, place it on the throat and chest before going to bed. Cover it well.

Four or five drops of turpentine in a spoonful of sugar and taken before bedtime.

Hattie Hill

Skunk oil is taken internally for croup.

David Atkinson

Vaseline given in doses ⅛ of a teaspoon every few minutes until relieved is a sure cure.

Mrs. J. T. Benson, Sr.

Mix and cook some bees wax, turpentine, and tallow. Dip a cloth in it and put on the chest to help croup.

Mrs. Harold Hudson

Turpentine is a sure remedy for croup. Saturate a piece of flannel with it, and put on chest, and in a severe case three or four drops on a lump of sugar may be taken inwardly.

Old Columbus, Georgia
Newspaper, 1880

Stand the child up beside the wall and take a knife and cut a notch even with the top of the child's head and as soon as the child grows above that notch it won't never have the croup no more.

Henry Burk

Nine drops of kerosene on sugar is a cure for croup.

Charles L. Price

Fill teaspoon with sugar and drop several drops of kerosene on it. This will help a person who has a bad cough or croup.

Mix several large spoons of snuff with water and make a paste. Spread this paste on a clean cloth and apply to chest.

Dissolve one teaspoon alum in one pint of honey. This can be given as needed for cough.

Mrs. Callie Knowles

A piece of fresh lard as large as a butternut, rubbed up with sugar in the same way that butter and sugar are prepared for the dressing of puddings, divided into three parts and given at intervals of twenty minutes will relieve any case of croup which has not already progressed to the fatal point.

Sore Throat, Miscellaneous

To get rid of the sore throat, boil a chicken gizzard and drink the water from this.

Negro maid

Black pepper is often mixed with salt for the sore throat.

Mrs. Lewis Newton

For a sore throat tie your old dirty sock around your neck.

Mrs. Herman Greene

Gargle for sore throat
Make a tea of red oak bark, with a little alum dissolved in it.

Sue Peacock

For hoarseness
To a pint of whiskey add as much rock candy as it will dissolve. Use; a teaspoonful at a time.

Sue Peacock

Tonsilitus
Take a wool cloth and put in a frying pan then add tar tallow and beeswax and let them melt, and let soak into the cloth. Bind this tightly around the neck.

Mrs. H. C. Harper

Take a jawbone of hog, break it and take marrow. Rub it on throat, good for tonsilitus.

Rebecca Porter

Chills
At bedtime, drink a pint of hot grape wine, sweetened with a spoonful of sugar.

Dr. J. A. Brock

Sinus
Chew a small amount of honey comb (or one tablespoon). Take honey comb every hour at least for four to six hours. Chew each amount for about ten minutes and spit out the remaining part.

Cecilia Colquitt

Chewing sweet gum from a sweet gum tree is good for the lungs. It strengthens weak lungs.

Mrs. J. M. Thompson

Put tallow on the bottom of a baby's feet to unstop his nose.

Mrs. Dalton Thomley

Appendix

FOLKLORE AND FOLKLIFE: COLLECTION, DOCUMENTATION, PRESERVATION

Bringing in the Harvest

All of us are inescapably linked with the life and lore of our folk. To collect and study folklore is to know ourselves, to put us in touch with our fellowman, to share in—not preserve as quaint anachronisms— our tales, songs, riddles, recipes, superstitions, and rhymes. To experience the folk mind unconsciously as an inheritor and transmitter is to be one of the folk; to experience it intellectually is quite another thing. Nearly all folklore collectors have written of this dichotomy, have been perplexed and befuddled by it, and some have feared it, but none have failed to be humbled and freshened by the folk who nurture traditions which lay such strong hold on our hearts and minds. Quite apart from these philosophical and psychological considerations, collecting folklore is a lot of fun, and most of us could do with a good bit more of that. Once you start, you can't stop, and before you know it, you've dragged neighbors, friends, kinfolks, and utter strangers in with you, and all sorts of really fine things happen to everybody.

There are several ways to collect folklore: the collector may simply write down the substance of an item, whether tale, riddle, rhyme, or song, a method valuable for the recording and presentation of verbal folk archives; he may, additionally, write descriptive and biographical sketches of the informant, his surroundings, and the interview, often casting the account into the language of the informant; he may use the tape recorder, camera, and motion picture not only to document a specific item but also to capture the entire event, whether an interview or a festival. All these methods have inherent advantages. The collection of verbal archives is simplest; written accounts satisfy in the way good books always do; and mechanical equipment enables us to enter fully into the actual folk experience. Depending on his inclination, finances, equipment, and purpose, the collector will find the method or methods best suited to him.

All these methods are used at Foxfire, a center of folklore collection, study, and publication in Rabun Gap, Georgia, where a group of high school students, led by B. Eliot Wigginton, Esq., has achieved national prominence. Foxfire, originally funded by the National Endowment for the Arts and Humanities, now a financially independent corporation, is engaged in photography, film making, recording, folk architecture, the restoration of folk buildings and the re-creation of a nineteenth-century community, and the assembly of folk archives, including a museum. Four books of folklore and folklife studies have been published: The *Foxfire Book* in 1972, *Foxfire 2* in 1973, *Foxfire 3* in 1975, and *Foxfire 4* in 1977 (all by Anchor Press-Doubleday, all available in hardcover and flexbound volumes). The texts, authentic and fresh, enriched by excellent photographs and drawings, focus (1) on domestic crafts—the actual processes, skills, and tools involved in hog killing, moonshining, weaving and quilt making, log-cabin and chimney construction, the making of wagon wheels, soap, chairs, baskets, and musical instruments; and (2) on cultural phenomena such as faith healing, burial customs, and midwifery. There appear also, from time to time, collections of remedies, recipes, superstitions, and ghost tales. One of the best features of the *Foxfire* series is the interview with local people who exemplify folk traditions. Energetic and dedicated, the students of Rabun Gap and their inspired teacher have shown the rest of the country not just a way to collect folklore, but a philosophy of collecting. They present their folk with pride, they have kept faith with folk traditions, and they, the young, have brought credit to themselves and to the old, whose lives they have closely touched and honored.

Two other multimedia centers for the collection, preservation, and dissemination of folklore are the Center for Southern Folklore at Memphis, Tennessee, and Appalshop at Whitesburg, Kentucky. The Center for Southern Folklore is involved primarily in the production and distribution of very fine films about American folk life, and it is currently assembling a folklore archive. Recently, the Center published *American Folklore Films & Videotapes: An Index*. Appalshop, which began as an OEO community film workshop, now sponsors a quarterly, *The Mountain Review;* a community center, The Loft, where activities include film making, video, photography, cable television, a series of recordings and the performing arts—threatre, dance, and music; and Roadside Theatre, a traveling players' group that retells mountain tales and offers dramatizations of folklore. Their films on coalminers, midwives, one-room schools, church services, and folk crafts are widely distributed, and many of them have been showcased in the Museum of Modern Art in New York. The Appalshop tale-tellers are a splendid group who, without scenery, props, or costumes, have done much to restore the folktale to its rightful place in America. In Alabama, they have performed for audiences in prisons and correctional centers with the full support and cooperation of the Alabama Board of Corrections, and at Alexander City State Junior College. Appalshop has delighted theatre audiences in our nation's capital and in New York.

That the tape-recorded interview can be used brilliantly by the folklorist is attested by the success of Theodore Rosengarten's *All God's Dangers* (New York: Alfred A. Knopf, 1975). This first-person narrative by a Reeltown Negro is as interesting for its authentic folk speech, its delineation of the rural Alabama Negro as he was in the first half of the twentieth century, its descriptions of the skills and implements of agriculture during that period, and its evocation of an entire folk culture, as it is for its broader historical, economic, and political aspects.

The camera, both still and motion picture, provides visual insights into folklife and folklore. *Down Home*, a photographic study (with accompanying text) of Camden, Alabama (photographs by Bob Adelman and text by Susan Hall; New York: Quadrangle, The New York Times Book Co., 1972) is a very good example of the use of photography as a medium for the recording of both history and folklife. Katherine Tucker Windham's recent publication *Alabama: One Big Front Porch* (Huntsville: Strode Publishers, 1975), a survey of Alabama folk traditions, including the legends of Steve Renfroe and Railroad Bill, is enhanced by both H. Roland Russell's drawings and the author's photographs.

Most persons who are interested in folklore do not have the resources of Appalshop or Foxfire. How does one collect on a spare budget, short on funds for film, camera, even gasoline?

First, the collector might try to enlist the aid and interest of local civic, literary, professional, garden, and business organizations in a specific folklore project, one with definite, limited aims, say, a 16mm film on a group of folk musicians or a craftsman. The PTA might be willing to pay for a short printed collection of folk games, riddles, and sayings from elementary school children; a literary club might be convinced to purchase a tape recorder for a high school English class to use in the collection of folk tales. The county historical association could perhaps sponsor a photographic survey of historic folk buildings. A church could involve its membership, both young and old, in the restoration of a cemetery and the collection of gravestone carvings and inscriptions. The association of the amateur collector with various volunteer groups like Scouting, 4-H, and Future Farmers of America can lead to all sorts of profitable ventures in folklore collecting.

If all these semi-organized efforts fail, purchase paper, pencils, and pens, and go it with a friend or two. Start in your own backyard, attic, kitchen, and front porch with family, friends, and neighbors. The technique is simple: You listen, they talk. If you are genuinely interested in your informant as a person, not just as a source of folk tradition or as a specimen of folk life, the response will be, invariably, warm and full. People enjoy telling their tales, singing their songs, remembering their pleasures and hardships, exhibiting their skills. They do it naturally, often with great flair, without a trace of pretension or shyness, and always with a fine awareness of the thing itself, be it a riddle or a hog killing. Be careful to note correctly the name and address of the informant, to ask for his permission to use the material, and to offer copies of the results of your collection. If you do not know the informant, find somebody who does and can go with you or send word ahead that you're coming. If the informants are children, secure the permission and assistance of their guardians, teachers, or parents. In addition to the interview and the folk stuff that are transmitted orally, the collector should be aware of such sources as letters, diaries, journals, account books, personal papers, legal documents, church and community histories, scrap books, proceedings of local legislative bodies, and old newspapers. All these may contain either items of folklore or interesting accounts of the folk life of older generations.

The old people of America are a rich, enormous, and largely untapped source of our folk traditions. Nearly every town has an existing organization of those over sixty-five. In Tallassee, Alabama, the 65+ Club meets several days a week for hot lunch and hours of quilting. Their lovely quilts, all of traditional American design, provide revenue for sight-seeing trips to such places as Yellowstone National Park and Disneyland. In 1964 they traveled to Washington, where they presented a quilt to President Lyndon B. Johnson, and in the spring of every year they host the state meeting of 65+ Clubs—an all-day to-do of exhibits, swap-outs, singing, dancing, and fiddling. Their efforts are completely voluntary, they receive no subsidies from any agency, and they are a lively group, actively engaged in continuing their folk traditions. The would-be collector would do well to "spend the day" with 65+'s, and stir their vivid memories of the past.

The collector, then, must carry tape recorder, camera, pencil, paper, whatever he can and chooses, on his jaunts. More important, he must be undaunted by August heat, brambles, nettles, mosquitoes, fire ants, sudden thunderstorms, freezing winds, and unmapped country roads. On some days all creation will conspire against him, and he will come home with two or three scraps for hours of labor, bone-weary and despairing. Somebody will tell him of an ancient, venerable graveyard and he drives a hundred, two hundred miles to find that the tombstones and graves have all been removed to make way for a new interstate or flooded by a new dam. He is directed to a raconteur of great wit and broad range, but when he gets there he is told that so-and-so died last week. Often, though, he goes looking for the pot of gold and finds instead buried greenbacks. One thing leads to another; a fellow may not know the right road to Mt. Hebron, but he sends you on to Robinson Springs and the tombstone of Alabama's first governor. Or the would-be collector loses his way in the hills of Tallapoosa

County, it's nearing sunset, the peanut butter sandwich he ate at noon is wearing out, no store or house sighted for miles, and suddenly, rounding a bend, he sees against the crimson sky a startlingly beautiful white frame country church. The 1858 bell still rings pure and sweet, and a cemetery full of inscriptions awaits him.

Richard Dorson describes his experience in collecting the folktales of Southern blacks transplanted to Michigan, in his book *American Negro Folktales* (Indiana University Press, Harvard University Press, 1956, 1958; reissued, including earlier collections *Negro Folktales in Michigan* and *Negro Tales from Pine Bluff, Arkansas, and Calvin, Michigan,* by Fawcett, paperback). Dorson's adventures are typical of the failure, success, turn-around, go-sideways cycle which plagues the collector. Expecting much, he finds little; not even looking for anything, he stumbles on jewels, as we stumbled on Mrs. Ruth Herren—in the last phases of the preparation of our folklore volumes, we happened on a folklorist's dream, a gracious, spirited lady who picks a banjo and sings nearly all the folk songs of Alabama. Collecting is often a matter of such happenstance.

The classic personal account of folklore collecting in America is John Lomax's *Adventures of a Ballad Hunter* (New York, Macmillan, 1947). Lomax, who, along with his son Alan, was responsible for the deposit of over 600,000 folksongs in the Library of Congress, writes of many a chance encounter with singers like Leadbelly, Clear Rock, Captain Nye, Sin-Killer Griffin, Black Samson, and, in Alabama, Dock Reed, Rich Amerson, and Enoch Brown. And in these present volumes of Alabama folklore, the collections of students at Troy State University were largely determined by uncontrolled circumstances: student collectors just "happened" to find certain informants at particular times. And so, much of what appears here came by Fate, a force the folk themselves recognize and to which they pay tribute in some of their games, songs, sayings, and tales. We hope such fortunate accidents befall other present and future collectors of folk traditions.

Serving up the Feast

Inasmuch as the actual substance of folklore is not widely available to the public, although accessible to scholars and teachers, what is there for the general reader who is interested in the subject?

The anthologies of Benjamin Botkin, though attacked by some scholars who felt that the editor included too much pseudo-folklore, are, in the main, good sources of all the genres represented in American folklore:

Treasury of American Folklore (Crown Publishers, 1944)
Treasury of Southern Folklore (Crown Publishers, 1949)
Treasury of New England Folklore (Crown Publishers, rev. ed. 1949)
Civil War Treasury of Tales, Legends, and Folklore (Random House, 1966)
Treasury of American Anecdotes (Crown Publishers, 1966), one of the best
    general collections of American folk humor.
Lay My Burden Down: A Folk History of Slavery (University of Chicago Press,
    1945), one of the first printed volumes of the slave narratives collected under
    the WPA folklore project.
The American Play Party Song (Frederick Ungar, 1963), an encyclopedia of
    game, dance, and play-party songs from Oklahoma.

Duncan Emrich is foremost among American scholars who have
made folklore collections attractive to the general public: to date, he
has edited several popular volumes for children and adolescents and
an excellent general anthology, *Folklore on the American Land* (Little,
Brown, 1972), which includes sections on American names (cattle
brands, fiddle tunes, race horses and hound dogs, quilts, and mining
camps, nicknames and place names), riddles, rhymes, street cries and
epitaphs, legends and tales (urban folk tales, Jack tales, Gullah tales,
and legends of such assorted folk as Jesse James, Santa Claus, and
George Lyman Kittredge), folk songs (historical, cow-country, sea
shanties, love songs, and murder ballads), and folk beliefs and superstitions. Emrich, like John Lomax and Carl Sandburg, writes about the
American folk and their lore with irresistible warmth and shamelessly
open affection, and all his books provide comprehensive bibliographical citations. His *American Folk Poetry* (Little, Brown, 1974) is a superb
collection of American folk songs gathered from the Archive of Folk
Song in the Library of Congress.

Tristram P. Coffin and Henning Cohen have edited two important
general collections:

Folklore in America (Anchor Books, 1970, reprinted from hardbound edition by
    Doubleday in 1966), a wide-ranging collection, in both geographical and
    ethnic distribution, of superstitions, tales, proverbs, songs, tales, riddles,
    games, folk dramas and festivals, all gathered from the pages of the *Journal
    of American Folklore*, the informants and the collectors carefully noted, and
    motifs and types assigned to the tales according to the universally accepted
    Stith Thompson and Antti Arne designations.
Folklore From the Working Folk of America (Anchor-Doubleday, 1973), a very
    fine anthology of folklore from archives and journals of folklore: tales and
    anecdotes of the workers and laborers of America—rhymes, jump rope
    chants, riddles, jokes (mostly current knock-knock, "sick," and shaggy
    elephant jokes), home remedies, superstitions of actors, soldiers, and min-
    ers, folksay (street cries, nicknames, parodies), games (a good section on
    current adolescent kissing games), folk festivals, including the half-time

homecoming show at Georgia Tech, legends like Casey Jones and Johnny Appleseed, and, of interest to Alabama readers, a treatment of "Railroad Bill," the legend retold by Margaret Gillis Figh, folklorist at Huntingdon College, first printed in *Southern Folklore Quarterly*, and three songs about the outlaw-hero, one with musical notation.

Other well-known collectors and collections include:

Vance Randolph:
  Ozark Folk Songs, 4 vols. (Columbia, Mo. State Historical Society, 1946–1950)
  Ozark Folk Tales (1951–1958)
Richard Chase:
  The Jack Tales (New York: Houghton Mifflin, 1943)
  Grandfather Tales (New York: Houghton Mifflin, 1949)
  American Folk Tales and Songs (New American Library of World Literature, 1962)
John A. and Alan Lomax:
  Collections of American folk songs including *American Ballads and Folk Songs* (New York: Macmillan, 1938)
  Our Singing Country (New York: Ludlow Publishing Co., 1941)
  Folk Song: U.S.A. (New York: Duell, Sloan, & Pearce, 1947)
  Folk Songs of North America (Garden City, N.Y.: Doubleday, 1960)

The Frank C. Brown Collection of North Carolina Folklore (Seven volumes, Durham: 1952–1964) is particularly noteworthy as one of America's outstanding regional collections. Professor Brown was an ardent collector and teacher of folklore at the University of North Carolina. At his death, Professor Newman I. White, who earlier had made a substantial collection of Alabama folklore while he was teaching at Alabama Polytechnic Institute, assumed the general editorship of the hitherto unpublished Brown materials; nine specialist editors ultimately contributed to the final published volumes. White's general introduction offers not only a discussion of Professor Brown as a collector, his involvement with the formation of the North Carolina Folklore Society, and his relationship with John Lomax who was, at that time, directing the WPA efforts in the collection of American folklore, but also a well articulated, if brief, philosophy of folklore, especially in the realm of systematic comparative studies. Volume one is an anthology of folk games and verbal lore; the games and rhymes, edited by Paul Brewster, are remarkably similar to those we have found in Alabama; the riddles, 290 from 69 contributors, are edited by Archer Taylor, who organized them according to form and structure; the proverbs, also edited by Taylor and derived from four separate collections, including one that the playwright Paul Green made for WPA, are very fine, and the discussion of substance, imagery, place and personal names is most illuminating; the section on folk speech, edited by George P. Wilson, is arranged alphabetically with extensive quotations, the emphasis primarily antiquarian and linguistic; legends and tales, edited by Stith Thompson, are short specimen narratives which exhibit common motifs, the most impressive a tale of a traveller transported to the realm of Betsy Longtooth and her sister witches. Four volumes of the Frank C. Brown collections are devoted to folk songs and ballads: *Folk Ballads* (vol. 2), *Folk Songs* (vol. 3), both edited by H. M. Belden and Arthur Palmer Hudson, both issued in 1952, and *The Music of the Ballads* (vol. 4), and *The Music of the Songs* (vol. 5), both edited by Jan C. Schinhan and published in 1964. Volumes 6 and 7, *Popular Beliefs and Superstitions from North Carolina,* issued 1961–1964, are edited by Professor Wayland D. Hand, who here emerges incontestably as the foremost scholar in this area of American folklore. His intent that the North Carolina collection become a reference work is fully realized; citations to analogues are copious and Professor Hand's classification system is now standard.

There are several fine anthologies of folklore as it surfaces in literature: one of the best is *Folklore in American Literature* edited by John T. Flannagan and Arthur Palmer Hudson (White Plains, New York: Row, Peterson, 1958), which contains a selection of folk songs and works by Zora Neale Hurston, Vance Randolph, Carl Carmer, and J. Frank Dobie, as well as literary uses of folklore in Hawthorne, Poe, Washington Irving, Joel Chandler Harris, Longfellow, Frost, Sandburg, Faulkner, and Alabama's Johnson J. Hooper.

The folklore associated with children ought to be studied in connection with Mother Goose, and there are two very fine reference works here: Ceil and William S. Baring-Gould's *The Annotated Mother Goose* (Clarkson N. Potter, 1962; also a 1967 Meridian paperback), a guide to the sources and history of nursery rhymes, to various collections, editions, and illustrations; and *The Oxford Dictionary of Nursery Rhymes* (Oxford University Press, 1951) edited by Iona and Peter Opie. An older but still good collection of children's literature, which presents a comprehensive collection of Mother Goose rhymes, riddles and folk verse, and literary folk tales, in addition to fiction and poetry, is *Anthology of Children's Literature,* edited by Edan Johnson, Carrie E. Scott, and Evelyn R. Sickels (New York: Houghton Mifflin, 1935, 2nd ed. 1948), still in wide use as a college textbook.

The following introductory studies are especially useful to the beginning student of folklore:

Jan Harold Brunvand's *The Study of American Folklore: An Introduction* (W. W. Norton, 1966) contains discussions of all folklore genres, notably clear definitions and classifications, valuable chapter bibliographies, and an appendix on the architecture of the log cabin.

Standard Dictionary of Folklore, Mythology, and Legend, ed. Maria Leach, 2 vols. (New York: Funk & Wagnalls, 1949–1950).

Kenneth and Mary Clark's *Introducing Folklore* (New York: Holt, Rinehart & Winston, 1963) has a section on the survey and discussion of childlore.

Tristram Coffin's *Our Living Traditions: An Introduction to American Folklore* (New York: Basic Books Inc., 1968) is a collection of essays by prominent American folklore scholars on methodology and major areas of study: ballads, lyric folk songs, Negro folk songs, musical structure and notation of folk songs, folk dance, magic, folktales, legends and tall tales, folk games, the trickster hero, proverbs, riddles, superstitions and folk beliefs, folk speech, the hillbilly movement, the folklore of laborers, twentieth-century Negro music, blues, gospel, and jazz.

Richard Dorson's *American Folklore* (Chicago: University of Chicago Press, 1959) includes sections on Colonial Folklore, with emphasis on witchcraft and the white man's relationship with the Indian; The Rise of Native Folk Humor, 1790–1865, as reflected in newspapers, almanacs, and paperbound sketchbooks, with particular mention of Lincoln the yarnspinner; Regional Folk Cultures, the Pennsylvania Dutch, the Ozarks, Spanish New Mexico, the Mormons of Utah, and the Yankees of Maine; Immigrant Folklore, old world customs, beliefs and practices in America; The Negro, a history of the collection and study of Negro songs, spirituals, music, tales, and beliefs; A Gallery of Folk Heroes, Davy Crockett, Paul Bunyan, Gib Morgan the story teller, John Henry, Johnny Appleseed and Jesse James; Modern Folklore, treating of "jokelore," practices on the college campus, and G. I. folklore.

Bibliographies in American folklore and folk song are issued by the Library of Congress, Archive of Folk Song, and are available at nominal or no charge, upon request. Tristram Coffin's *An Analytical Index to the Journal of American Folklore* (Publications of the American Folklore Society, Bibliographical and Special Series, vol. 7, 1958) is helpful in locating specific studies and collections published in the JAF, and Charles Haywood's *A Bibliography of North American Folklore and Folksong* (New York: Dover Publications, 1962) will also be of use to the student and to the general reader who wishes to locate an area of interest. The Library of Congress also issues numerous authentic recordings of American folk song and folk tales, all of them moderately priced, catalogs available on request. The series prepared in connection with the American Bicentennial Celebration is particularly good. High school and community libraries ideally should purchase some of these Library of Congress recordings. Our national museum, the Smithsonian, since its inception has fostered research in American folklore and life—among the most successful exhibits prepared for the Bicentennial were those which re-created our folk history, the nineteenth-century post office and apothecary shop, and an early

American home in construction. From time to time, the Smithsonian sponsors travelling shows of folk art, and the series of folk festivals held on the Mall have been extremely popular with the public.

The empress of all American folklore quarterlies is the *Journal of American Folklore*, a publication of the American Folklore Society, founded in 1888 and now published at the University of Texas. The society itself is distinguished in its membership, and international in its affiliations. Other publications of the Society include: *Abstracts of Folklore Studies, The American Folklore Newsletter*, and a series of publications ranging from reprints of essays and bibliographical volumes to book-length studies, and yearly supplements which report the proceedings of annual meetings. The American Folklore Society cooperates with the Modern Language Association in the compilation of folklore bibliography, with the Smithsonian Institution, and with the Library of Congress. The *Journal* itself is a forum for American folklore scholars; though its contents are highly specialized, the general reader will enjoy looking it over. Most of the essays are devoted to scholarly analysis and debate, quite often international in scope and character; yet the *Journal* also addresses itself to contemporary public issues related to folklore and now and then prints the results of a field investigation. Collections limited or pertinent to textual criticism are also printed, and the Society encourages (and lists in its supplements) the formation of folk archives throughout the country. Each issue contains reviews of current books, recordings, and films in folklore. The JAF is indexed in the *Social Sciences and Humanities Index to Periodicals* and *The Book Review Index*. Back copies are available to libraries and individuals through special order. Subscription is automatic with membership in the AFS.

One of the oldest and most important scholarly periodicals in folklore is the *Southern Folklore Quarterly*, published by the University of Florida in cooperation with the South Atlantic Modern Language Association. Like the *Journal of American Folklore*, it prints studies on every aspect of folklore, sometimes devoting an entire issue to a particular subject; for example, the June 1975 issue on African and Afro-American folklore reports the results of field studies, reviews full-length volumes, and includes a field collection. Among the journal's important functions as a center for the publication of folklore scholarship is the annual bibliography issue, which indexes both articles and full-length studies appearing in both Spanish and English in the Western Hemisphere.

Other well-known folklore periodicals include: *The Folklore Forum: A Communication for Students of Folklore*, Folklore Institute Indiana University; *Journal of the Folklore Institute*, edited at Indiana University; *Journal of the Ohio Folklore Society*, Bowling Green State University; *Keystone Quarterly*, The Pennsylvania Folklore Society; *Kentucky Folklore Record*, Kentucky Folklore Society, Western Kentucky State College; *Louisiana Folklore Miscellany*, Louisiana Folklore Society, Louisiana State University; *Mississippi Folklore Record*, Jackson; *North Carolina Folklore*, North Carolina Folklore Society, North Carolina State University at Raleigh; *New York Folklore*, New York Folklore Society, Cooperstown; *Pennsylvania Folk Life*, Pennsylvania Folklore Society, Lancaster; *Tennessee Folklore Society Bulletin*, Tennessee Folklore Society, Middle Tennessee State, Murfreesboro.

Since the foundation of the American Folklore Society, according to the Library of Congress listings, 133 organizations devoted to the collection and preservation of folklore and folksong have been established. Some are statewide, others county and community. Among them are: Arkansas Folklore Society at the University of Arkansas; Bucks County Folksong Society, Langhorne, Pennsylvania; California Folklore Society at San Fernando Valley State College; Folklore Society of Greater Washington, Washington, D.C.; Kansas Folklore Society, Wichita State University; Kentucky Folklore Society, Bowling Green; Michigan Folklore Society, University of Michigan at Ann Arbor; New York Folklore Society at Cooperstown; Mississippi Folklore Society at Decatur; North Carolina Folklore Society at Raleigh; Ohio Folklore Society at The Ohio State University; Pennsylvania Folklore Society, University of Pennsylvania; Hoosier Folklore Society, Folklore Institute, at Bloomington, Indiana; Tennessee Folklore Society, Murfreesboro; Texas Folklore Society; and the Virginia Folklore Society at the University of Virginia.

Folklore is now a respectable academic discipline in American colleges and universities, with the University of Texas, Indiana University, the University of Pennsylvania, the University of Florida, UCLA, and the University of North Carolina being among the leaders in collection, archives, publications, and course offerings. The state of Virginia, historically, has been a great center of folk song study, the Mississippi Folklore Society is among the most active of all such organizations in the South, and Arkansas and the Ozarks are well represented in the studies and collections of Vance Randolph. The monumental Frank C. Brown Collection of Folklore in North Carolina has placed that state foremost in archives and publication. It was at the University of North Carolina that W. T. Couch, regional director of the Federal Writers' Project, achieved such great success with the "life histories" undertaking by the WPA. American universities are repositories of folklore and folklife archives; the Library of Congress lists forty-five states which possess such archives. Among those universities are the University of Arkansas; the University of California at Berkeley, Los Angeles, and San Diego; Georgia State University; Southern

Illinois University; the University of Illinois; Indiana State University; and the Universities of Mississippi, Massachusetts, Kentucky, Idaho, North Carolina, New Mexico, Pennsylvania, Texas, and Virginia.

Folklore was collected on a massive national scale in America during the thirties with the Works Progress Administration. Under the Federal Writer's Project, Folklore Division, hundreds of collectors gathered folk songs, folklife, folklore, life histories, and slave narratives, county by county, state by state. William F. McDonald in his full-length study *Federal Relief Administration and the Arts: The Origins and Administrative History of the Arts Projects of the Works Progress Administration* (The Ohio State University Press, 1969) has documented carefully both the idea of government subsidy for the arts and the actual complex evolution of those agencies—state, national, and regional—which implemented and sustained programs ranging from mural painting to marionette theatres. Professor McDonald's book meets a long-felt need not only in general American historical researches but also in the history of American arts and literature. Drawn entirely from original source materials, the official correspondence, memoranda, and records of the WPA and personal interviews, his study details the philosophy of white collar social and economic relief, the genesis and early concepts of the arts subsidy idea, the legislative and presidential structuring of the arts phase of WPA, budget and finance, organization of national and state offices, and the operation of the Federal Theatre Project, the Federal Music Project, the Federal Writers's Project, and the Historical Records Survey. The state of Alabama, incidentally, provided a model for the rest of the nation in the assembly of archives and history. Dominated by the idea of a series of "guides" to all the states, the National Writers Projects underwent sharp conflict with state and local offices that were interested in other writing efforts. The Folklore Division, first led by John Lomax, whose interests lay primarily in the South and Southwest, under Benjamin Botkin swiftly inaugurated procedures for collection. The results of those collections are now housed at the Library of Congress and in various state and university archives. How little of the material was actually published is indicated by Professor McDonald's book. If the original aim of the Folklore Division was to make the general American public aware of our folk heritage through publications of the collections, the purpose has not yet been fulfilled. Obviously, editing and publishing such a great amount of material will be a giant undertaking, equal to that of the initial collection.

In years past, local newspapers and regional almanacs and gazettes disseminated folk tales, riddles, rhymes, proverbs, remedies, folk wisdom, and wit to the literate public. (Scholarship in this area is generally inadequate: extensive collections of folklore could and ought to be made from early American newspapers and periodicals.) The local newspaper is now, more often than not, mostly advertisement and local news, but there is no reason why it cannot once more serve as a forum for folk reminiscences, legends and tales, anecdotes and pranks, songs, sayings, and superstitions. Jesse Culp's column "Down to Earth" in the Sunday *Birmingham News* and the current series of articles written by Henry Willet under the sponsorship of the Alabama Arts Council, which feature folk craftsmen, musicians, and other folklore and which appear in several Alabama community newspapers, are steps in that direction.

Folklore studies are naturally and properly linked with history. For the Alabama folklorist whose interest is primarily historical or for the student who is inclined to place his collection and researches within the broader study of Alabama history, there are several significant works. Not the least of these are various county and town histories, which, unfortunately, are not in wide distribution. Usually, these may be obtained by application to local community and school libraries, the county historical association, the Judge of Probate, private individuals, or the Alabama Archives. Personal accounts, sketches, and essays like Mitchell B. Garrett's *Horse and Buggy Days on Hatchet Creek* (The University of Alabama Press, 1957) and Viola Goode Liddell's *With a Southern Accent* (University of Oklahoma Press, 1952) are useful, as are courthouse records, private journals, letters, proceedings of town council meetings, and newspapers of state and county circulation. A. B. Moore's *History of Alabama* (Tuscaloosa: Alabama Book Store, 1951), though it has fallen under attack from many quarters, is still valuable. The latest historical study is Virginia Van der Veer Hamilton's *Alabama: A History* (W. W. Norton, and American Association for State and Local History, 1977), part of the States and the Nation Series prepared in connection with the American Bicentennial Celebration. A brief list of other interesting historical and social studies would include also: James Benson Sellers, *Slavery in Alabama* (The University of Alabama Press, 1950), Charles Summersell, *Alabama History for Schools* (Birmingham: Colonial Press, 1957), Clarence Cason, *90° in the Shade* (University of North Carolina Press, 1935), Lucille Griffith, *Alabama: A Documentary History to 1900* (The University of Alabama Press, 1972), Carl Carmer, *Stars Fell on Alabama* (Farrar & Rinehart, 1934), and *Alabama: Mounds to Missiles* by Helen Morgan Akens and Virginia Pounds Brown (The Strode Publishers, rev. ed. 1972).

Readers interested in folk material culture—in those items that are the actual stuff of Alabama folk life—will want to visit the Pike County Pioneer Museum in Troy, where, under the leadership of Mr. Curren Farmer, an outstanding collection has been assembled. The collection of farm implements, though as yet uncatalogued, is particularly fine; in addition to the two main buildings which house the collection, there are an authentic log cabin and a country store which were moved to the museum site. The museum held its first crafts festival in 1973, and folk life and craft events are scheduled regularly—spinning, fiddling, and Sacred Harp singing. Pike Pioneer Museum is attracting visitors from all over Alabama and neighboring states. It is certainly well worth visiting.

Another fine small museum of folk and historical items is located in Loachapoka, Alabama, on Highway 14, near Auburn. The entire town of Loachapoka has been placed on the National Register of Historical Places, and the museum itself is housed in a building preserved and renovated by the Lee County Historical Society. The Museum issues several small publications, holds fairs in September and June, and in conjunction with the Homecoming Association sponsors an annual Homecoming Dinner-on-the-ground formerly held at the splendid old Loachapoka Methodist Church, which, tragically, was destroyed by fire in 1977. Readers interested in these activities should get in touch with Mr. Alexander Nunn of Loachapoka, former editor of *The Progressive Farmer* and guiding light of the preservation efforts in that old Alabama settlement.

Several county courthouses are being transformed into folk and historical museums by various groups of citizens and historical associations, and there are a number of such centers operated by individuals—for example, Ma'Cille's in Gordo, Pickens County, the Mize-Western museum in Clayton, and the one operated by Mr. Tatum Bedsole in Geneva County. Alabamians are becoming increasingly aware of the importance of preservation and restoration of homes, hotels, and larger town buildings, and some effort, largely under the Heritage Farm Program, is being expended on identifying and preserving smaller or utilitarian folk structures—smokehouses, barns, blacksmith shops, well houses, privies, and outbuildings. Church and school buildings of great value to the historian and folklorist are being destroyed or deserted. The current inventory of property now being conducted by the State of Alabama for purposes of tax assessment offers an excellent opportunity for some enterprising soul who might identify those folk structures on a county-by-county basis.

The student of folklore and the student of history have much to offer each other, as the museums at Troy and Loachapoka visibly demonstrate. While every county in the state, and some towns, can boast of a historical association, there are no corresponding folklore organizations. We found one reference to an Alabama Folklore Society in 1893, but so far have been unable to substantiate it. County folklore associations could and ought to be organized either within existing local historical societies or under their auspices. As Foxfire has so success-fully demonstrated, the study and collection of folklore can and ought to be incorporated in the high school curriculum. Awareness of our folk traditions can begin in elementary and middle schools with dramati-zations and stories of our folk past, with demonstrations of folk crafts and arts, and with folksongs. The community college, the local library, volunteer civic, professional, and women's clubs, church groups, and organizations like 4-H and FFA, all have a stake in Alabama folklore. We hope that our volumes of Alabama folklore will motivate the establishment of many new, enthusiastic efforts in stimulating aware-ness of Alabama folk life and lore.

Acknowledgments

Our thanks to go to—

The staff of the Thomas Russell Library of Alexander City State Junior College, especially Mrs. Joyce Robinson, Mrs. Eula Hardaway, Mrs. Mary Nell Jenkins, Mrs. Peggy Causey, Mr. Bob Schrimser, and Mrs. Frances Tapley, whose assistance in research and bibliography expedited the completion of this work; and to the librarians, wherever they are, who answered our calls for help, especially Dr. Ruth Fourier of the Ralph Draughon Library of Auburn University for her encouragement, faith, and prompt action.

Dr. John Brewton, folklorist, author, anthologist, and professor emeritus of George Peabody College for Teachers, Nashville, Tennessee, who first encouraged the collection and organization of a folk profile of Alabama, and who graciously read the original manuscript.

Dr. James W. Byrd of East Texas State University and Dr. James Ward Lee of North Texas State University, who read and encouraged the publication of this material.

The late Dr. Emmett Kilpatrick of Camden, Alabama, and the Troy State University we knew as Troy State Teachers' College, who inspired, advised, and encouraged us in all matters academic, folk, and human.

Dr. R. C. Kennedy, also of Camden, Alabama, who encouraged, and continues to encourage both of us, and who read our marriage vows and touched our children with the holy words and water of baptism.

Janice Riley, Brenda Corley, Sharon Atkinson, Phyllis Hornsby, Lily Roberts, Larry Hornsby, and other typists who labored with us.

Dr. W. Byron Causey, president of Alexander City State Junior College, and Dr. Charles Farror, dean of the faculty, Alexander City State Junior College, for all sorts of valuable assistance and encouragement necessary in the pursuit of this book.

Mr. James Travis, at The University of Alabama Press, for the faith that fathered publication.

Dr. Curtis Wayne Sellers, The University of Alabama, for his assistance.

Mr. Rick Sellers, for research on our behalf in the Library of Congress.

Mr. William Lower, for advice, patience, and technical assistance.

Senator John Sparkman for his many efforts in our behalf.

Miss Sarah Ann Warren of the Alabama State Department of Archives and History, for her help in assembling archives.

Mr. Joseph Hickerson and Mr. Gerald Parsons of the Library of Congress, Archive of Folk Song, for their assistance in locating and procuring research materials.

Dr. James C. Ray, who read the remedies.

Our student collectors over the last twenty years, and the hundreds and hundreds of informants, who are really the authors of this work.

Our families, "unto the sixth generation," for providing us with a rich inheritance of folk knowledge and understanding.

Our children, Jacqueline, Suzannah, and Will, who followed us, complaining
and protesting sometimes, perhaps, but who nevertheless followed us to
churches, cemeteries, family reunions, and down unfamiliar roads looking
for . . . something.

Contributors

Adams, Mrs. Bell

Adams, Faye

Adams, Irene

Adams, Oyette

Adams, Mrs. Robert

Adams, Mr. & Mrs. Roy

Adkison, Joan

Aldrich, Grace

Allen, Betsy

Allen, Ella Kate

Allen, Mrs. Minnie

Allen, Mrs. Pauline T.

Allen, Ruby

Allen, Sara

Ammerman, Claude Tom

Amos, Mr. Mac

Andalusia High School
Student Body

Anderson, Johnny

Anderson, Mrs. J. W.

Anderson, Mr. Tommy

Anderson, Vicki

Andress, Bobby

Andress, Mack

Andrews, Jerry

Andrews, Perlie

Atkinson, David

Avery, Mr.

Bailey, Mr. Bill

Bailey, Mrs. Drew

Balkcon, Mrs. Donie

Balkom, Faye

Ballard, Mrs. Loreli

Bane, Janice

Barefoot, Bill

Barfoot, Fred

Barnes, Mrs. Carolyn

Barnes, Mrs. E.M.

Barns, Miss Darly

Bass, Fletcher

Bass, Mary

Bates, Joe

Baxley, Nena

Beard, Mrs. J.J.

Bedsole, Mr. F.B.

Bedsole, Mrs. Mattie N.

Bedsole, Tatum

Belcher, Mrs. Lillian

Belcher, Penny

Bell, Mrs. Major

Bender, Elsie

Bennett, Carol

Benson, Sr., Mrs. J. T.

Bentley, Vicie

Benton, Mrs. John

Benton, Mr. & Mrs. Tom

Berry, Elizabeth

Best, Jasper

Biddie, Mrs. Lee

Birch, Mrs. Nellie

Black, Lucie Mae

Black, Mrs. Lula

Black, Olene

Blackstock, Mr. Allen

Blackstock, Mrs. C.M.

Blackstock, Cleone P.

Blackwell, Barbara

Blackwell, Mrs. Josie

Blair, Daisy Mae

Blake, Annie

Bledsole, Johnny

Bodenstein, Cal

Bonds, Patricia

Bonner, Annie Brice

Bonner, Henry

Bonner, John Dale

Bonner, Joseph Lee

Booker, Mrs. Amos

Booker, Mrs. E.W.

Booker, Linda

Boone, Cynthy

Booth, Ila

Borom, Mrs. Leslie

Boswell, Hazel

Boswell, James

Bowen, Patsy

Bowers, Miss Martha Jo

Bowman, Barron

Bowman, Betty

Boyd, Dr. G.R.

Bozeman, Ken

Bozeman, Matt

Bozewell, Eleanor

Brackin, Mrs. Bob

Bradley, Cathryn

Bradley, Mrs. Lum

Bragg, Zelda

Breeden, Danny

Brewton, Mark

Bridges, Mrs. Allene

Broadaway, Mrs. Major

Brock, Dr. James A.

Brock, James Carl

Brooks, Bammer

Brooks, E.C.

Brooks, Mr. J.W.

Brooks, Mrs. J.W.

Brooks, Mrs. Ola Bell

Brown, Eugene

Brown, J.T.

Brown, Mrs. J.W.

Brown, Lowell

Brown, Mrs. L.G.

Brown, Miss Patti

Brown, Patricia

Brown, Yvonne

Broyant, Mrs. Ruby

Brunner, Miss Henri

Bryan, Mrs. Fannie

Bryan, Yvonne

Bryant, Ruby

Bucklew, Faye

Bundy, Ella

Burdeaux, Esther

Burk, Henry

Burkett, Alvin

Burkett, Cecelia

Burkett, Fannie

Burks, Nellie

Burks, Robert Turner

Burnett, Emmy

Burnett, Mr. W.B.

Butler, Leui

Byrd, Mr. H.L. Jr.

Byrd, Mrs. L.E.

Byrd, Mary Olive

Caddali, Charlie

Caldwell, Myra

Calloway, Mrs. Eunice

Campbell, Adeline

Campbell, Alice

Campbell, Mrs. Estella

Campbell, J.D.

Campbell, Leonard

Campbell, Lois

Canady, Thomas

Canales, Duane

Cargile, Fannie

Carroll, Dale

Carroll, Mrs. Lewis

Cassady, Clara

Causey, Mrs. O.G.

Cavley, Willie Dord

Chance, Liby

Chaney, Susan

Chapman, Mrs. Lucy

Chavers, Carl

Cheatham, Mrs. Gus

Cheatham, Jean

Cherry, Mr. G.P.

Chestnut, Effie

Chestnutt, M.M.

Chisumn, Donna Kay

Clark, Mrs. Aleen

Clark, Lola

Clark, Pearl

Clary, Betty

Clemmons, Marilyn

Clepper, Mrs. L.D.

Clipson, Dr. William

Clower, Dola Bell

Cobb, Mrs. Ola

Coker, Terry

Cole, Mrs. Annie

Cole, Liz

Cole, Mrs. Winston

Coleman, Mr. B.R.

Coleman, Mrs. Mary

Coleman, Mrs. Tom

Collins, Mr. Feston

Colquitt, Mrs. Cecil

Colquitt, Cecilia

Conner, Anne M.

Conner, Carolyn E.

Conner, Claud H.

Conner, Frances

Conner, Francis

Cooper, Annie

Cope, Ada Cameron

Cope, James Ruben

Cope, Mrs. James R.

Copeland, James

Copelone, Lola

Cotter, Nola

Countryman, George G. Jr.

Cox, Mrs. H.E.

Cox, Mrs. Ralph

Coxwell, Mrs. Rozelle

Crenshaw, Savannah

Crittenden, Mrs. Margaret

Crittenden, Mr. Zack

Crittenden, Mrs. Zack

Crosby, Mertle

Crosby, Pop

Crutchfield, Mr. Lonnie

Culpeper, Jonnie May

Culpeper, Mrs. Robert

Culver, Mrs. Ashley

Dale, J. Carlisle

Dale, Laura Estelle

Daley, Mrs. William

Danford, Mrs. Nancy

Daniels, Grace

Daniels, Pearl

Daniels, Walter

Dann, I.L.

Dansby, Geral

Dansby, Merle

Darby, Alice

Darden, Mrs. Georgia

Darman, Mrs. W.R.

Daughtery, Mrs. Weida

Davis, Bonnie

Davis, Mrs. Earl

Davis, Florence

Davis, Larry

Davis, Linda

Davis, Lonnie

Davis, Mary

Davis, Wallace

Davis, Willie

Day, Maggie

Day, Mrylene

Deal, Grace

Dean, Bonnie

Dean, Don

Dean, Evelyn Bonner

Dean, Isaac

Deithman, Bobbie

DeJarnette, Susan

Deloney, Linda

Dendy, Cerric

Deuce, John

Dewberry, Bobby

Dismukes, Mrs. Willis

Dismukes, Miss Willie

Dix, George Allen

Dixon, Don

Dixon, Fostelle

Dixon, Linda

Docket, Mattie

Dominy, Mrs. M.M.

Donaldson, All

Donaldson, Charles

Donaldson, Griffin

Donaldson, Mrs. Elizabeth

Donaldson, Mrs. R.R.

Dorch, Mrs. Dora

Dorsey, Donna

Dorsey, Henrianne

Downing, Maggie

Dozier, Mrs. Mabel

Drake, Lola

Driver, Mr. Andrew

Duke, Mrs. J.H.

Duncan, Clyde

Duncan, Mrs. Opa

Dunn, Mr. George

Dunn, Marie

Dunn, Mrs. T.L.

Dunn, Mrs. W.E.

Dyess, Eliza

Dyess, Ken

Dyess, Mavis

Dyess, Maybell

Eason, Rice (family)

Eddings, Glenda

Eiland, Mrs. Peggy

Eiland, Mrs. Virginia

Elderidge, Mrs. Epsy

Eldridge, Wayne

Ellis, Gail

Ellis, Mary Ann

Ellison, Mrs. F.L.

Ellison, Lizzie

Elmore, Carolyn

Emfinger, Sarah

Evans, Becky

Evans, Betty Sue

Evans, Henry

Evans, Johnny

Evans, Mrs. Truman

English, Bobbi

English, Nellie

Ernst, Mrs. L.R.

Eubanks, Sue

Everett, Martha Lou

Faincloth, Mrs. Rubye

Fannin, Joe

Farmer, Mrs. Charlie

Farmer, Mrs. Tom

Felts, Mrs. Clint

Ferguson, Charles

Fields, Tom

Fleming, Mrs. A.L.

Fleming, Mrs. Alice

Fleming, Gail

Flowers, Jimmie

Flowers, Sara

Floyd, Annie

Floyd, Ronnie

Floyd, Susan Collier

Foley, Mrs. Fred

Foley, Mary

Folman, Mrs. Stewart

Fondern, Mammie

Fonnen, Joe

Fordham, Jerl

Forester, Miss Celes

Forman, Mrs. W.B.

Formly, Mr. M.S.

Fowler, Hilda

Fowler, J.D.

Foy, Miss Sallie Mae

Franklin, Mrs. Clinton

Franklin, Mrs. L.H.

Freeman, Estelle

Freeman, F.M.

Freeman, Fish

Freeman, Mary Lynne

Fuller, Nadine

Gafford, Mrs. E.

Gaines, Grace

Gaines, Ivy

Galloway, Bud

Gantt, Mr. A.B.

Gantt, Eva

Gantt, George

Gantt, Mary Ann

Gantt, W.B.

Garcia, Dorothy

Garret, Nellis

Garret, Sherri

Garrie, Mrs. Tommie

Gates, John W.

Gavin, Linda

Gavin, Maylene

Gay, Rev. & Mrs. George

Geiger, Mrs. Eloise H.

Geiger, Mr. & Mrs. H.H.

Geiger, Rebecca

German, Mrs. Claudia

Geshagan, Miss Nancy Matilda

Gibbons, Wayne

Gibson, Bascom

Gibson, Mrs. Joe

Gibson, Martha B.

Gilbert, Miss Sara Doris

Gill, Huel

Gillion, Hanna

Glass, Lola

Glass, Mrs. Mary Will

Gober, Miss Sue

Gober, Mr. L.F.

Godwin, Mrs. J.A.

Godwin, W.E.

Godwin, Mrs. Will

Goff, Mrs. Jim

Goodman, Effie

Goodson, Mrs. Mattie

Goolsby, Mrs. C.W., Sr.

Goolsby, Bill

Goolsby, Janie

Gordon, Mrs. W.W.

Gorrie, Mrs. Tommie

Grace, Mr. George

Granes, W.C.

Grant, Emma

Grantham, Ann

Grave, W.C.

Greathouse, Dorothy

Green, Jean P.

Green, Stanley L.

Greene, Herman

Gregory, Mrs. Frances

Gregory, Glenda

Gregory, Peggy

Grey, Mrs. Willard

Griffin, Max

Griffin, Merma

Griffith, A. Jack

Grimes, Beaman

Grimes, Mr. Bemus

Grimes, Charles

Grimes, Mr. Lucious

Grimes, Mrs. Ruth

Grisset, Irene

Griswold, Ira

Griswold, Lilla Mae

Griswold, Martin

Griswold, Rebecca

Gubbard, Benny

Gulbreth, Mrs. Eunice

Gullege, George

Guy, Curtis

Hagan, Gail

Hagan, Mr. Gaston

Hagan, Loretta

Hagan, Mrs. Violet

Hair, Mrs. Byron

Hair, Mrs. Sara

Hall, Carolyn

Hall, Mrs. Ed

Ham, Mr. & Mrs. James H.

Ham, Mrs. Mable

Hammock, Mrs. Mary

Hancock, Maggie

Hankins, Mrs. J.H.

Hanson, Mrs. Nan

Harbuck, Nelda

Harlor, Mrs. A.J.

Harper, Mrs. H.C.

Harrell, Frances

Harris, Mrs. Clyde

Harris, Lois

Harris, William Peyton, Sr.

Harrison, Mildred

Harrison, Ruby

Harrison, Mrs. Willie

Hart, Mrs. Maggie

Harvey, Mrs. W.R.

Hataway, Mr. Morris

Hataway, Mrs. Sudie

Hatcher, Artie

Hattaway, Mrs. Bert W.

Hayes, Eva

Hayes, James Preston

Hayes, Mrs. Minnie

Haynes, Gladys

Heartfield, Mrs. Ellen

Heceims, Lula E.

Heileman, David Sr.

Heilman, Irene

Helms, Deborah

Helms, Harold

Helms, Peggy

Helms, L.P.

Helms, Mrs. T.L.

Henderson, Mr. Harvey

Henderson, Patricia

Henly, Mr. Steve

Henry, Otis

Herren, Mrs. Ruth

Hickman, Mr. & Mrs. J.C.

Hicks, Mary Glenn

Hill, Hattie

Hilson, Mrs. Joe

Hines, Kate

Hines, Mattie

Hinson, Russ

Hinton, Gale

Hodges, Mrs. J.W.

Holiday, Mrs. George

Holland, Mrs. Mae

Hollis, Annabel

Hollis, Emma Lou

Holloway, Mrs. Alice

Holman, Eliose

Holman, Mr. H.L.

Holmes, Vera

Holt, Mrs. Ella

Holt, Mrs. Johnny

Horath, Mrs. Lois

Horn, Mr. Beresford

Horn, Mrs. Edd

Horn, Mrs. Ray

Horn, Mrs. Selma Bailey

Horne, Ginny

Hornsby, Mrs. Amanda

Hornsby, Belinda

Hornsby, Mrs. Eric

Hornsby, Mrs. Ida

Hornsby, Joe

Hornsby, Lynn

House, Mrs. Elise

Howard, Jim

Howard, Mrs. J.C.

Howell, Mrs. Arizona J.

Howell, Jim

Howell, Martha

Hudson, Mrs. Harold

Hudson, Mrs. J.C.

Hudson, Mary Jo

Huges, Demarius

Huggins, Mary

Hughes, Mrs. Emmanette

Hughes, Mrs. Randolph

Hughes, Wanda

Hughes, L.R.

Huleman, Patricia

Hullen, Mrs. Maggie

Hunley, Eula Mae

Hussey, Mrs. Low

Hutchensen, Mrs. Dora

Hyde, Mrs. Annie

Inman, Fae

Ivey, Leah

Ivey, Mrs. Richard

Jackson, Mrs. Minnie B.

Jackson, Mrs. Susie

Jackson, Roberta

Jacobs, Edward Earl

James, Willie

January, Louise

Jarvis, Mrs. B.M.

Jarvis, Dr. J.C.

Jay, Ruby

Jenkins, Henry

Jenkins, Liza

Johns, Mr. Homer

Johns, Mr. Joe

Johnson, Aimie

Johnson, Mrs. Anne Floyd

Johnson, Curtis

Johnson, Mr. Dan

Johnson, Mrs. Eulska

Johnson, Mrs. Fred

Johnson, Mrs. Helen

Johnson, Mr. J. Carrol

Johnson, Liza

Johnson, Mozell

Johnson, Mr. Ollie

Johnson, Mrs. Pauline

Johnson, Mrs. Sarah

Johnson, Mrs. W.R.

Joiner, Mrs. Gussie

Jolly, Mrs. Louise

Jones, Bob

Jones, Exa

Jones, Jewel

Jones, Judy

Jones, Natalie

Jones, Judge Walter B.

Jordan, Hattie

Keeling, Betty

Kelly, Fannie

Kelly, Faye

Kendrick, Claude

Kendrick, Cullen

Kendrick, Era Andress

Kendrick, John Ray

Kendrick, Lorena

Kendrick, Roy Crowe

Kennedy, Carla

Kennedy, Thomas

Kent, Mrs. Kirby

Kilpatrick, Hiram

Kilpatrick, Mrs. O.S.

Kilpatrick, Miss Pat

Kimbo, Fannie

King, Mrs. Maggie

King, Mrs. S.J.

King, Mr. Will Sr.

Kinke, Miss Ginny

Kinsauld, Jackie

Kirkland, Mrs. C.E.

Kirkland, Clarence

Kirkland, Mrs. John

Kizzar, Maggie

Klumpp, Minerva

Knight, Josephine

Knowles, Mrs. Callie

Lake, Mrs. E.M.

Lake, Ethel

Lamberth, Mrs. R.E. Sr.

Land, Mr. Roy L.

Langford, Mrs. J.T.

Lansdon, Marciline H.

Lansford, Erclene

Lawrence, Elaine

Lawerence, Mrs. Ora Lee

Lee, Biddie

Lee, Miss Elenor

Leverette, Mrs. Minnie

Lewis, Miss Annie

Lewis, Esker

Lewis, Mrs. Eunice

Lewis, Mr. J.C.

Lidale, Mrs. W.R.

Liddell, Viola G.

Lightfoot, Lucille

Liles, Mrs. Myrtle

Liles, Sylvia

Limbert, Mrs. Nancy

Lipham, Mrs. Myrtie

Livingston, Mrs. C.T.

Locklar, Annie Mae

Locklar, Lois

Locklar, Pat

Lodgins, Mr. Jim

Lovejoy, Tom

Lowry, Martha

Mack, Mrs. E.R.

Mack, Mary

Mackmiller, Kathleen

Maddox, Charles

Maddox, Mary

Mahone, Bertha

Mahone, Wm. Fletcher

Majors, Mrs. Della

Malloy, Melynda

Mann, Mrs. B.R.

Mann, Mrs. Espy

Marler, Hazel

Marsh, Mr. Travis

Marshall, Carolyn

Martin, Mrs. Dixie

Martin, Mrs. J.D.

Martin, Martha Kate

Martin, Norma Jo

Marvin, Mary Evely

Marwell, Mrs. Iris

Massey, Helen

Mathis, Patsy

Mathison, Mrs. Addie

Matteson, Maurice

Matthews, Dorothy

Matthews, Fannie

Matthews, Mrs. George Jr.

Maughon, Lynn

Maughon, Theda

Maughon, Timmie

May, George

McCall, Mrs. Nadine

McCall, Tom

McCart, Linda

McCart, Mrs. Zach

McCarty, Frankie

McClendon, Hilda

McCleod, Mrs. Zuleika

McCormick, Mr. Sam

McCullough, Lurlean

McDaniel, Margie

McGill, John

McGowan, Mrs. Lawerence

McInnis, Margaret

McKenzie, Eva

McKinnon, Elizabeth

McLellan, Mr. Alphonso

McLellan, Lillie G.

McLendon, Lorine

McLure, Mr. S.E.

McMurphy, Mrs. George

McMurray, Mrs. W.H.

McNeill, Mrs. Joe

McPherson, Gordon

McVay, Julia

Medley, Mrs. James

Medley, Mrs. Men

Meek, Mrs. C.J. Jr.

Merrill, Henry

Merrill, Mellessa

Merritt, Mary Glenn

Messer, Betty

Messick, Mrs. Cummy

Messick, Lurlene

Metcalf, Mrs. Florine

Metcalf, Mrs. Malzie

Metcalf, Martha

Metcalf, Mattie

Metcalf, Mr. W.F.

Miller, Jack

Miller, Mae

Mills, Baltimore

Mills, Carol Lee

Mills, Hattie Mae

Mills, Joe

Missildine, Meluin L.

Mitchell, Donald

Moates, Mrs. Speller

Money, Mrs. Frank

Moody, Mrs. Thelma

Moore, Bud

Moore, Mrs. I.U.

Moore, Mrs. J.M.

Moore, Kathryn

Moore, Mrs. Robert

Moore, Mrs. Ruby

Moreman, Mrs. George

Morgan, Alice

Morgan, Marilyn

Morris, Curtis

Morris, Dean

Motley, Lucille

Mott, Mr. Will

Moulder, Jane

Murphy, Mrs. Lillian

Murphy, Cora Mae

Murray, Lillie

Myers, Mrs. Gene

Napier, Miss Sue

Nash, Mrs. A.S.

Neely, Mrs. Tom D.

Nelson, Carolyn

Nelson, Frances

Nelson, Mr. & Mrs. H.B.

Nelson, Mrs. J.S.

Nelson, Mrs. Lola

Nettles, Mrs. T.B.

Newell, Leacy

Newton, Mrs. Lewis

Nichols, Miss Barbara

Nichols, Dot

Nichols, Mrs. T.J.

Nolan, Mr. Hullen

Norman, Phillip

Norrell, Harriette

Norrell, Robert

Norris, Bob

Norris, Christine

Norris, Corine

Norris, Mrs. Jeff

Norris, Luvada

Norris, Mary

Norris, Maye P.

Norris, Susie

Norsworthy, Mrs. M.W.

Odom, Mr. Archie

Oswald, Jack

Owens, Buna

Owens, Mr. Sam

Owens, Sylvia

Padgett, Joann

Padgett, Mrs. Montene

Page, Mrs. Lee

Parker, Brenda

Parker, Buddy

Parker, Joe

Parker, June

Parker, Lamar

Parker, Mrs. Lula

Parker, Mrs. Ruth

Parker, Mary L.

Parks, John

Parks, Mrs. Ruth

Parmer, Floy

Parmer, Mr. Marvin

Parramore, Mrs. D.D.

Parson, Mrs. Ann

Parsons, Mr. D.E.

Partridge, Mrs. C.F.

Passmore, Miss Elenor

Patterson, Mrs. A.L.

Patterson, Mrs. Levon Jr.

Patterson, Mrs. Mabel

Paulk, Larry E.

Payne, Jim

Peacock, Miss Claire

Peacock, Rachel

Peacock, Sue

Peebles, Linda

Pennington, Mr. Gerald

Pennington, Mrs. Mamie

Perkins, Mrs. Evie

Perry, Annitta

Perry, Clyde

Perry, Rosa

Peters, Lorene

Petrey, Mrs. Jane

Petrey, Mrs. Howell

Phillips, Jimmie Sue

Phillips, Mrs. Lee

Phillips, Mae

Pickson, Mr. Jeff

Pickson, Mrs. Jeff

Pienezza, Mrs. Mackie

Pierce, Judy

Pierce, Tod

Plant, Reuben

Porter, Rebecca

Powe, Mamie

Powell, Mr. Emmett

Powell, Linda

Presnell, Mr. J.C.

Presnell, Mrs. J.G.

Prestwood, Mrs. Emmie

Price, Charles L.

Price, Mrs. Maye

Price, Rosemary

Price, Sam

Pride, Mrs. Charles

Pridgen, Sula

Pritchett, Mary Ann

Purnis, Wayne

Quant, Mrs. Ralph

Raines, Mrs. Willie

Ralph, Mildred

Ramsey, Gussie L.

Reeder, Mrs. Vassie

Reeves, Clarde M.

Reeves, L.V.

Reeves, Mrs. Mae

Reeves, Merton

Reeves, Mrs. W.G.

Register, Bertha Mae

Respress, Mr. D.A.

Reynolds, Rose

Reynolds, Sandra

Rhodes, Lorenza

Rhodes, Mrs. Louzina

Richards, Caroline

Richards, Minnie

Richards, Sally Pearl

Richardson, Joyce

Riggsley, Dr. & Mrs. Ernest D.

Rinhart, J.A.

Robbins, Shirley

Roberson, Friendly

Roberts, Leo

Roberts, Ken

Roberts, Luna

Rodes, Annette

Rogers, Mr. Benny

Roling, Jimmy

Rooker, Anne

Rozelle, Eddie

Rushing, M.O.

Russel, Bob

Russel, Mr. Robert

Russell, Mrs. Everett

Russell, Mrs. Willie Mae

Salter, Freddie

Sanders, Carl

Sanders, Mrs. Fannie

Sanders, Jernigan

Scarborrough, Mr. Albert

Scay, Mrs. Sallie

Schlich, Maybelle

Scofield, Mrs. Perry

Scofield, Thomas

Scott, Bobby Paul

Scott, Henry

Screws, W.O.

Seay, Mrs. Sallie

Sellers, Mr. A.E.

Sellers, Patsy

Serials, Mrs.

Sessions, Anna Rose

Seymore, Mattie

Sharpless, Mr. Red

Shaw, Rita

Shields, Jim

Shields, Lizzie

Shiver, Mrs. Willie

Sightler, Carl

Sikes, Floyd

Silverthorne, Lana

Simmons, Mrs. Odessa

Singletory, Mrs. Bill

Sipper, Mr. B.A.

Sloan, Mrs. Gladys

Smart, Aliene

Smart, Jace

Smith, Mrs. Arabelle

Smith, Bennie Frank

Smith, Carlton

Smith, "Uncle" Charlie

Smith, Mrs. Claude

Smith, Mrs. Gertrude

Smith, Johnny B.

Smith, Lily

Smith, Mrs. Mary Ann

Smith, Mary Pat

Smith, Rena May

Smith, Sue

Snell, M.L.

Snell, Tallulah

Solomon, Ellen

Solomon, Mrs. M.H.

Somerset, J.A.

Spivey, Jake

Stacy, Mrs. Faye

Staggers, Olene

Stanford, Mr. Lee

Starling, Dot

Steele, Mrs. Eunice

Stephens, Mrs. Frank

Sterkx, Mr. H.E.

Stewart, Sarah

Stewart, Stevie

Stokes, George

Stokes, Mr. & Mrs. Lee

Street, Major

Strength, Mr. L.L.

Strength, Mrs. "Murt"

Strickland, Alice

Strickland, Webbie

Stroud, T.M.

Summerford, Patsy

Suttle, James Parke

Sutton, Ann

Sutton, Sherrie

Swain, Mrs. Nita

Tam, Phoebe

Tate, Willie

Tatum, Ame

Tatum, Lena

Taylor, Cleatus

Taylor, Florence

Taylor, Sidney

Taylor, Sonja

Taylor, Mrs. Willie C.

Terrill, John

Terry, Jerry

Terry, Mrs. Pauline

Thaggard, Mr. O.L., Sr.

Thomas, James

Thomas, Liz

Thomas, Mrs. Louise

Thomas, Mrs. Mamie

Thomas, Pat

Thomas, Paul

Thomas, Phylis

Thomas, Mrs. Sharon J.

Thomas, Sherel

Thomas, Mr. Walter

Thomas, Mr. Wendell D.

Thomley, Mrs. Dalton

Thompson, Altha

Thompson, Ben

Thompson, Mrs. J.M.

Thompson, Josie Cora

Thompson, Murry

Thompson, Mrs. Myrna

Thompson, Bobby

Thornton, Glenda McLean

Thrash, Mrs. Laurie

Threat, Mrs. Willie

Throyer, Mrs. Lois

Tillman, Mrs. B.T.

Tindall, Mrs. Maynard

Tisdale, Mrs. Beth

Tolbert, Mattie R.

Tracy, Priscilla M.

Traweek, Miss Eugenia

Traweek, Miss Gertrude

Traweek, Mr. Jimmy

Trawick, Dixie

Treadway, Janice

Turley, Robert

Turner, Carolyn

Turner, Laura Elizabeth

Turner, Ernest

Turner, Mr. Oby

Turner, Ruby

Tye, Ruth

Vaughn, Marcy

Vickery, Henry D. Jr.

Wade, Minnie

Walding, Cheryl

Walker, Mrs. Ham

Walker, Mrs. Otis

Waller, Lan

Ward, Miss Callie

Ward, Glenda

Ward, Mrs. Missouri

Ware, Ann

Ware, Mr. Mose

Warley, Mr. O.C.

Warley, Mr. W.C.

Warr, Miss Janey

Warren, Mary Ellen

Wasden, Mary Alice

Watford, Lula

Watford, Mamie

Watford, Mrs. Minerva

Watkins, Mr. & Mrs. A.D.

Watson, Louise

Watson, Mrs. Myrtle

Watts, Bessie

Webb, Mrs. Margaret

Weed, Mrs. Marie G.

Weed, Sula

Weeks, Louise

Weeks, Mr. Robert H.

Wells, Mrs. Agnes

Wells, Mrs. G.K.

Whaley, David

Whaley, Tex

Whatley, Mildred

Whigham, Mrs. Julian

White, E.Z.

White, Mrs. Margie

White, Pearl

White, Sylvia

Whitehurst, J.D.

Whitman, Mrs. Jim

Whittle, Linda

Widow, Louzina

Wigham, Frances

Wigham, John

Wikle, Mrs. Ora

Wiland, Abner

Wiley, Mary Ann

Wilkins, Belle

Wilkinson, Mrs. Howell

Wilkinson, Mr. J.C.

Wilkinson, Patsy

Williams, Barbara "Bob"

Williams, Mr. Charles

Williams, Glen

Williams, Lewis

Williams, Mrs. Mary

Williams, Mary

Williams, Maylo

Williams, Oleae

Williams, Mrs. Phil

Williams, Mrs. R.E.

Williams, Stevie

Williams, Miss Wanda

Williams, Mrs. W.H.

Williamson, Mrs. Mary Americus

Willis, Eva

Willis, Hattie Mae

Wilson, Chris

Wilson, Dan

Wilson, Darwin

Wilson, Della

Wilson, Mrs. Ethylen

Wilson, Gertie

Wilson, Gladys

Wilson, Mrs. Guy

Wilson, Mr. & Mrs. James F.

Wilson, Johnny

Wilson, Joel

Wilson, Mary Katherine

Wilson, Mrs. Willis

Windham, Mrs. Carola

Windham, Mrs. Coddie

Windham, Edna

Windhamm, Kate

Wise, Mrs. Joe

Wood, Miss Wicke

Woodham, Mrs. John

Woodham, Johnnie

Woodham, Melinda

Woodham, Virginia

Wooton, Agnes

Wooton, Nora

Wright, Mr. W.T.

Wurley, Mr. O.C.

Yancey, Mrs. Elizabeth

Yarborough, Eva

Yarbro, Mrs. George

Yarbrough, Michael

Yeargan, Mrs. Mary Elizabeth

Yeargan, Miss Mary Jane

Yeomans, Ruby Joyce

Young, Epsie

Young, Lois

Young, Minnie

Young, Mr. Ned